English for academic study:

Speaking

Course Book

Joan McCormack
and Sebastian Watkins

University of
Reading

CALS
Centre for
Applied Language Studies

Garnet
EDUCATION

Credits

Acknowledgements

Published by
Garnet Publishing Ltd.
8 Southern Court
South Street
Reading RG1 4QS, UK

First Edition 2007
Reprinted 2008

ISBN: 978 1 85964 990 9

British Library Cataloguing-in-Publication Data
A catalogue record for this book is available from the
British Library.

Production
Project manager: Maggie MacIntyre
Editorial team: Emily Clarke, Richard Peacock, Rod Webb
Art director: Mike Hinks
Design and layout: Nick Asher
Illustration: Doug Nash
Photography: Clipart.com; Corbis; Digital Vision;
Getty Images; Mike Hinks; Stockbyte.
Audio: Matinée Sound and Vision

The present authors acknowledge their debt to Clare
Furneaux and Mark Rignall's *Speaking* (Prentice Hall, 1997)

Unit 5 Tasks 1 and 2, and Unit 10 derived from Furneaux,
C. and Rignall, M. (1997). *Speaking*. (Prentice Hall, 1997)

Every effort has been made to trace copyright holders and
we apologise in advance for any unintentional omissions.
We will be happy to insert the appropriate
acknowledgements in any subsequent editions.

Printed and bound
in Lebanon by International Press

The authors and publisher wish to thank the following
people or groups for permitting us to use or adapt their
material for use in *EAS: Speaking*.

Andalo, D. (2004, May 26). Employers urged to fight
obesity. *The Guardian*.

Author unknown. (2004, August 15). Men want to be
househusbands. Retrieved May 15, 2005, from
http://www.uominicasalinghi.it/index.asp?pg=1030.

Cook, L. and Martin, J. (2005, March 22). Chapter 2:
Households and families. In Social trends 35 2005 edition.
Retrieved May 20, 2005, from
http://www.statistics.gov.uk/socialtrends35/.

Garrat, B. and Francis, D. (1994). *Managing Your Own
Career*. HarperCollins Publisher Ltd.

Gerhardt, S. (2004, July 24). Cradle of Civilisation.
The Guardian.

Hill, R. (2004, June 20). How New Man turned into distant,
confused New Dad. *The Guardian*.

Hoare, S. (2003, August 26). E for Degree. *The Guardian*.

McGuire, R. (2004). Stress: Keep things in perspective.
Retrieved May 5, 2005, from http://www.pjonline.com/
students/tp2004/p18stress.html.

Pereira, H. Stay-at-home dads. Retrieved May 10, 2005,
from http://www.ivillage.co.uk/parenting/pracad/parcare/
articles/0,,186674_618693-1,00.html.

Revill, J. (2005, January 30). Singletons are on the increase.
The Observer.

Staff. (2004, January 24). Net Effects. *The Guardian*.

Woodward, W. (2003, February 22). Affluent but anxious
and alienated. *The Guardian*.

Woolfenden, J. (1990). *How to Study and Live in Britain*.
Northcote House.

The authors would like to add the following thanks.

Bruce Howell for materials and advice on Unit 6.

Anne Pallant, Bruce Howell, Colin Campbell, Frances
Watkins for suggestions, comments and proofreading of
early versions.

Chia Ling Lin (Kate), who gave feedback on trialling the
materials.

Contents

Book map

Unit	Topic	Skills focus	Language focus
1	Being a successful student	Delivering a presentation	Reporting back on a discussion Agreeing and disagreeing Using signpost expressions
2	Learning online	Participating in a discussion Recognising different perspectives Reaching a balanced conclusion	Summarising the outcome of a discussion Comparing perspectives Chairing a discussion
R	Review: Units 1 and 2		
3	Changing roles in the family	Presenting information from a text Anticipating arguments before a discussion	Referring to a text Exchanging opinions
4	A healthy lifestyle	Using a text to support your ideas Listening actively Exchanging information (1)	Clarifying and confirming understanding
R	Review: Units 3 and 4		
5	The influence of the media	Presenting information from charts Building on what others have said	Referring to data Referring to what previous speakers have said
6	Consolidation unit	Leading a seminar	Review and consolidation
R	Review: Units 5 and 6		
7	The world of work	Finding a focus for a presentation Preparing for a discussion by thinking the issues through	Taking turns in a discussion
8	Protecting the environment	Designing a questionnaire Participating in a debate	Expressing quantity
R	Review: Units 7 and 8		
9	Science and the paranormal	Presenting a research proposal	Expressing doubt/belief
10	Studying in a new environment	Exchanging information (2)	Review and consolidation
R	Review: Units 9 and 10		

Introduction

The purpose of this book is to help you develop the speaking skills you need to participate effectively in academic seminars and discussions, as well as to help you develop effective presentation skills.

Structure of the course

There are ten units in the book. Each of the units is topic-based, e.g., a healthy lifestyle, the world of work. The discussions and the presentations you make are related to the topic of each unit. The written or listening texts are designed to give you different perspectives on a topic, and also to help you give evidence to support your ideas, thus giving you practice in one of the essential features of academic life.

Units 1 – 5 are the core units. Each of these units covers aspects of both seminar skills and presentation skills.

Unit 6 is a consolidation unit where you have the opportunity to put all these skills into practice by organising your own seminars and discussions, and choosing your own topics. (Depending on the course you are taking, your teacher may decide that you begin these seminars earlier).

Units 7 – 10 give you further practice in these skills.

Review

Every two units are followed by a review, giving you the opportunity to reflect on what you have learnt.

Useful language

Each unit has a section on useful language, language related to the task you need to perform in each unit. You should try to use this language in the appropriate situations.

Learner diary

The Learner diary is a section at the end of each unit. The purpose of this is to get you to think about the process of learning, and the particular strategies you are developing. Having this awareness will help you to be more in control of developing your language skills.

When you are speaking in another language, you need to think of ideas and the language you need to express those ideas. This can be challenging. The book helps you with this in two ways:

- In many discussion activities in this book you are asked to think about and prepare what you are going to say. This can improve your performance. As you become more confident and competent in speaking in English, the need for preparation time should decrease.

- As it can be difficult to concentrate on both ideas and language, you are sometimes asked to focus on the ideas you want to express on a topic, and to discuss these. After the discussion, you are asked to look at, and sometimes practise, relevant useful language phrases (see above). Following this, you are required to return to the original topic, or a similar one, and discuss it again with different students, this time using the useful language.

What you put into the course will determine how much you get out of it. Obviously, if you want to improve your speaking, it is essential that you practise this skill, and you should prepare well for the sessions in class, as well as participating actively in them.

1 Being a successful student

In this unit you will:
- reflect on your experience of speaking in an academic context;
- analyse your strengths and weaknesses in speaking;
- identify and practise language for agreeing and disagreeing;
- consider aspects of a successful presentation;
- give a short informal mini-presentation.

Communicating orally in academic situations

There are a number of different situations in which you will need to communicate orally in English on your academic courses. The main situations are presentations, seminars and discussions. In academic culture, students need to clearly express their views on different issues related to their subject area. These views are often based on a critical reading and evaluation of written texts. The more you study and engage with your subject areas, the more your ideas will develop and change. This will help you to develop your critical thinking skills, which are a key part of academic study. It is also important that you develop the language skills that will enable you to express your ideas most effectively.

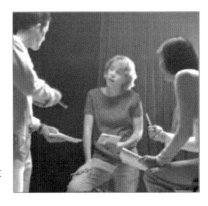

Task 1: Your experience of speaking English

1.1 Below is a list of some of the situations which require you to speak on academic courses. Which of them do you have experience of, either in your own language or in English? Put a tick (✓) in the appropriate box.

		English	Own language
a	Giving a formal presentation.		
b	Participating in a seminar (group discussion).		
c	Leading a seminar (group discussion).		
d	Discussing and giving your opinion in a seminar on pre-assigned articles you have read.		
e	Speaking with a department tutor in a one-to-one tutorial (e.g., about an essay plan).		
f	Discussing feedback on your written work with a tutor in a tutorial.		
g	Discussing your studies with other students.		
h	Other? (Please state)		

1.2 Compare your experiences with your partner. Give details of:

a) where you had each experience;

b) how it was structured (e.g., how many students were involved and how long the speaking turns were);

c) what kinds of topics you covered.

1.3 Now discuss which of the situations in Task 1.1 you find, or think you will find, the most difficult to do in English. Can you say why?

This course will help you develop the confidence and the skills necessary to participate effectively in the academic situations outlined above.

Task 2: Your attitude to speaking English

2.1 Look at the statements below. Do you agree or disagree with them? Which statements are important for you personally?

a) I want to speak English with a perfect native-speaker accent.

b) I want to speak English without a single grammatical mistake.

c) I feel as though I am a different person when I speak English.

d) My pronunciation is not as important as grammatical accuracy.

e) If I can communicate my meaning effectively, it does not matter if I make mistakes.

f) I don't like working in groups during English lessons because I may learn incorrect English from my classmates.

g) I want to speak English for social reasons as well as for academic reasons.

2.2 Form a group and discuss each statement. Do not spend longer than two minutes on each one.

2.3 Which statements were the most controversial in your group (i.e., caused the most disagreement)?

2.4 ⊕ Listen to the recording of some students reporting back on their discussion of the points listed in Task 2.1. Which of the statements do they refer to?

2.5 Now report back to the rest of the class on the most interesting/controversial points that came out of your discussion. Keep your report brief; include three to five points only. Try to use some of the *Useful language* expressions below for reporting back.

Useful language: Reporting back

Our group thought the most controversial point was …

Point X provoked the most discussion.

Point X was the most controversial point.

There was some disagreement about point X.

Some people felt …

Most of the group agreed …

Others disagreed …

2.6 Some of the words below may be useful for reporting back. Mark the stress on the following words:

discussion	controversial	disagreement	provoke

Seminar Skills: In seminar discussions, you may have to express agreement and disagreement with other students. In Task 3 you will practise using the language to do this.

Task 3: Agreeing and disagreeing

3.1 Read the statements below. Do you agree (A), disagree (D) or partly agree (P) with each one?

a) _____ If you want to succeed at university, you really need to manage your time well.

b) _____ It's important to do a lot of reading around before you choose a focus for your essays.

c) _____ The best time to revise for exams is just before the exam, when the pressure is on.

d) _____ The same study skills are necessary on both undergraduate and postgraduate courses.

e) _____ If you've completed an academic course in one country, you should be able to cope with a course in another country.

f) _____ People have different learning styles. It helps you learn more quickly if you're aware of how you learn best.

3.2 ⊕ Now listen to the recording of two students discussing these statements. Does the second speaker agree, disagree or partly agree with each statement? Underline the correct alternative in the *Opinion* column below.

	Opinion	Useful language
a	agree/disagree/partly agree	
b	agree/disagree/partly agree	
c	agree/disagree/partly agree	
d	agree/disagree/partly agree	
e	agree/disagree/partly agree	
f	agree/disagree/partly agree	

3.3 ⊕ Now listen again.

a) In the *Useful language* column above, write down the exact words the second speaker uses to agree, disagree or partly agree.

b) Try to say the phrases as they are pronounced in the recording.

3.4 Now look at the statements in Task 3.1 again. Work in pairs.

Student A: Read a statement.

Student B: Respond, using one of the *Useful language* phrases from Task 3.2. Give your own opinion and a supporting reason.

Task 4: Study skills for success

You are going to hear a conversation between two students, discussing the challenges of studying at a university. The female student is a native speaker of English. The male student is an international student who studied on a pre-sessional course.

4.1 🎧 Listen and number the points below according to the order in which the students discuss them.

_____ Plan ahead and begin working early.

_____ Choose areas to study that you are interested in.

_____ Find out what is important on your reading list.

_____ Ask a peer to read your work before submitting it.

_____ Use reading strategies to help you read quickly.

_____ Deal with stress by finding time for relaxation.

4.2 Can you add any more points to those mentioned in the recording?

Successful students   *plan ahead and begin working well in advance of deadlines.*

Successful students … _____

Task 5: Prioritising study skills

In small groups, you will now discuss the study skills you feel are the most important for success at university. You may use the ideas from the recording in Task 4.1, as well as your own ideas from Task 4.2 (*Successful students …*). Think about why they are important and come to an agreement about which five skills are the most important for your group. Later, you will need to justify these choices to the other groups.

Remember the language for agreeing and disagreeing from Task 3.

Presentation Skills: When giving a presentation, you need to help your audience follow your presentation by using signpost language. You also need to deliver your presentation clearly. Tasks 6 and 7 deal with these aspects of presentations.

Task 6: Tips for successful study – a mini-presentation

Now that you have looked at various aspects of being successful as a student, consider what advice would be useful for new students. You will give a mini-presentation to the class, explaining why the tips you chose are important.

6.1 Put your five points on an OHT or a poster. Remember to only include key words, not whole sentences. You will need to identify the key words for each of your tips for study.

6.2  Listen to the recording of a student presenting his top five study tips. Are any of the points the same as yours?

6.3 It is important to signal to your audience when you are moving from one main point to another. Look at the *Useful language* expressions from the recording for doing this.

Useful language: Signpost expressions

There are five main points which we consider important for successful study.

Our first point is …

Next, we have put …

Moving onto our third point, …

Fourthly, we think …

And finally, our last point is …

Note: Signpost expressions are important for:

- opening a presentation;
- guiding an audience through the main points;
- helping an audience understand the organisation;
- closing a presentation.

See Appendix 1 for a fuller list of signpost expressions.

6.4 The **content** of your presentation is very important; however, equally important is your **delivery**. If your audience cannot understand what you are saying, e.g., because your pronunciation is poor or because you speak too fast, then the content is wasted. Before you give your presentation, look at the points below, which are important aspects of delivering a presentation clearly.

- pronunciation of sounds and words
- intonation
- volume
- speed
- eye contact

6.5 Decide who will give the presentation; either one group member can give it or you can divide the presentation between two or more group members.

Practise your presentation in your group, concentrating on the points listed in Task 6.4. The other people in your group should give you feedback on these areas (e.g., "You need to make more eye contact with the audience.").

> **Presentation Skills:** Remember that presentation skills develop with practice. You will not do everything perfectly from the beginning, but feedback from your group can help you improve. Out of class, it can also be useful to record yourself. When you listen to yourself, you can sometimes immediately see possibilities for improvement.

6.6 Each group now gives its presentation to the whole class. Before you listen, look at the Presentation assessment form in Appendix 8a. You should fill in a separate form for each presentation (your teacher will give you copies). At the end of each presentation, compare what you noted on the assessment forms in your groups.

6.7 At the end of all the presentations, give each presenter the assessment form you filled in for their presentation. Read through the feedback you receive from other students.

6.8 Decide as a class which presentation was the best according to the criteria on the assessment form.

Task 7: A successful presentation

7.1 In addition to delivery, there are many other skills involved in giving a successful presentation. Would you consider the skills below good or poor? Put a tick (✓) in the appropriate box.

	Presentation skills	Good	It depends	Poor
a	The presenter puts as much information as possible on each slide.			
b	The presenter uses colour and sound to liven up their slides.			
c	The presenter reads from a script.			
d	The presenter memorises a script and recites it.			
e	The presenter uses notes.			
f	The presenter pauses after each main point.			
g	The presenter reads all the information on the slide.			
h	The presenter stands in one place all the time.			
i	The presenter speaks at the same speed all the time.			

7.2 Discuss your completed table in small groups.

Learner diary

Research into language learning has shown that reflecting on the process of learning has a strong impact on the effectiveness of how you learn. One way of doing this is through keeping a diary. This can either be a private diary, or you can show it to the teacher from time to time.

Before you fill in your first diary entry, complete the self-assessment questionnaire below.

Self-assessment of your speaking skills

Below is a list of a range of speaking skills Please indicate which of these you feel to be easy or difficult for you, where 5 means *I can do this well*, and 1 indicates *I do not feel competent at all*.

Speaking skill	1	2	3	4	5
I can speak accurately, without making too many grammatical mistakes.					
I can speak without hesitating too much.					
I can find ways to communicate my meaning, even if I cannot find exactly the right words.					
I can usually find the words I need to say what I want.					
Most people can understand my pronunciation.					
I can speak expressively with appropriate intonation.					
I can speak confidently in front of an audience.					
I can contribute effectively in group discussions.					
I can talk confidently in my own subject area.					

Now make an entry in your learner diary, thinking about your strengths and weaknesses in speaking English as identified in the self-assessment form above.

Learner diary

- What areas of speaking English do you feel you need to work on?

- What can you do to improve in these areas, either inside or outside the classroom?

- How do you feel about the speaking you have done so far in the lessons on this course?

Remember that thinking or reflecting on how you learn can improve the learning process.

Below is an example of a learner diary entry.

Learner diary 3rd July

I think my main problem in speaking is my pronunciation and my limited vocabulary. I also feel very nervous when speaking in front of the class. I did a presentation on good study skills in the speaking class and was really worried before I spoke. I think I need to do more practice of this type, so that I get more confidence. I also need to spend more time practising individual sounds - maybe I could do this in the language lab ...

2 Learning online

In this unit you will:
- identify characteristics of successful participation in discussions and seminars;
- consider problematic issues from different perspectives;
- practise summarising the outcome of a discussion;
- examine the role of a chairperson in a discussion.

Participating in seminars and discussions

On your future academic course you will need to participate in seminars and discussions with groups of other students. Usually you are expected to have done some preparation, e.g., read an article. These seminars take various formats. Some are led by tutors and others are led by students. In these seminars, you need to be able to state your viewpoint clearly and to develop the confidence to do this. This course will give you practice in participating in seminars, as well as giving you the opportunity to lead one.

Seminar Skills: It is important to think about how you can contribute effectively to a seminar. The purpose of Task 1 is to start you thinking about how you can do this.

Task 1: A successful participant in group discussions

1.1 Look at the list on the next page, which shows a variety of ways of behaving in a class discussion.

a) Mark a tick (✓) next to statements which are characteristics of:

a good participant (e.g., someone who is interested and active in the discussion);

a poor participant (e.g., someone who does not look interested and stays silent).

b) Be ready to give a reason for your answer.
If your answer is 'It depends', be prepared to explain further.

	The participant ...	Good	It depends	Poor
a	listens to what others say and builds on this, adding his/her opinion.			
b	tries to get other people to change their mind and agree with his/her opinion.			
c	always agrees with other people's opinions.			
d	does not say anything at all.			
e	explains his/her point in great detail, and at length.			
f	explains his/her points briefly.			
g	is nervous about speaking, but makes himself/herself do it.			
h	encourages others to speak, inviting them into the discussion.			
i	only speaks when asked.			
j	asks other students to clarify what they mean, or to explain further.			
k	changes his/her opinion during the discussion.			

1.2   Compare your answers with a partner, explaining the reasons for your choice.

1.3   What is considered good behaviour in group discussions in your own country? Do you think there are any differences from an English-speaking country?

Seminar Skills: In academic study, you need to look at issues from different perspectives, to think beyond your own experience or position. Considering issues from different perspectives is part of the process of reaching a balanced conclusion. Tasks 2 and 3 develop these aspects of critical thinking.

Task 2: Different perspectives on an issue

2.1   Look at this statement concerning education and consider it from the perspectives of the different people involved.

A seriously disruptive child should be excluded permanently from school.

What views might the following people have about the statement?

a) the teacher of the child

b) the parents of the child

c) the head teacher of the child's school

d) the child

e) the child's classmates

f) a child psychologist

g) the education authorities

2.2 Compare your ideas with your partner, giving reasons for the view of each person. Try to use some of the *Useful language* below for comparing perspectives.

2.3 ⊕ Now listen to a recording of a student comparing different perspectives on the statement in Task 2.1. What does the speaker say about the views of those involved?

Useful language: Comparing perspectives

From a (teacher's) perspective, …

From the point of view of (the parents), …

If I were (the head teacher of the child's school), I'd probably feel that …

The (child psychologist) would argue that …

Task 3: Reaching a balanced conclusion

3.1 Below are some other statements about school education.

Try to consider each one from the perspective of three or four different people who might be affected. Think about how the different people involved might view the issue. In addition to the people mentioned in Task 2.1, other people might include: university departments, future employers, society as a whole.

Try to think of long-term as well as short-term implications of the statements.

Statements

1   Corporal punishment is necessary to maintain discipline.

2   Children should be given formal tests and exams from the age of six.

3   Children should be allowed to leave school at 16 if they wish.

4   Parents should be allowed to educate children at home if they wish.

5   Children should be able to choose which subjects they want to study at the age of 15.

Use the table on the next page to record your points. Remember: at this stage, you are not recording your own views, but what you think the views of those directly involved might be.

Statements	Different perspectives			
1 Corporal punishment is necessary to maintain discipline.	Teachers: Many would support this as the only way to control large classes.			
2 Children should be given formal tests and exams from the age of six.				
3 Children should be allowed to leave school at 16 if they wish.				
4 Parents should be allowed to educate children at home if they wish.				
5 Children should be able to choose which subjects they want to study at the age of 15.				

3.2 You are going to discuss each of the statements from Task 3.1, comparing what you think the different views of those directly involved might be.

a) Compare the different perspectives for Statement 1 in small groups. Try to use some of the expressions from the *Useful language* box from Task 2.3.

b) When you have done this, give your own opinion on the first statement. What do *you* think should happen?

c) Compare your final opinion with the other people in your group. Are you able to agree?

d) Now repeat steps a) to c) for Statements 2 to 5.

Seminar Skills: In seminars, you may have to summarise the final outcome of a long discussion. Did people agree or disagree on the main issues, and why? What were the main points for and against? You looked at this in Unit 1, Task 2.5 (reporting back). Task 4 provides further practice in this skill.

Task 4: Summarising the outcome of a discussion

4.1 Listen to a student summarising a group discussion of the statement from Task 2.1 relating to the exclusion of disruptive children. Did the group agree or disagree with the statement?

4.2 Look at an excerpt of the student's talk below.

The phrases in the gaps show the speaker:

1 stating whether or not the group agreed;

2 acknowledging a strong argument against their final position;

3 qualifying their final position.

Listen again and fill in the gaps.

> This is a difficult question, but ❶ _____ that such a child should be excluded from school, as this would be in the best interests of most people concerned. ❷ _____ this action might cause some damage to the child's long-term ability to socialise effectively with other children, so we also agreed that ❸ _____ there is no other solution, I mean, if all else fails.

4.3 Now mark which words you think are stressed in each of the three phrases in the excerpt above. If necessary, listen again.

4.4 Next to each phrase in the following *Useful language* box there is a number. This number tells you how many words are stressed when this sentence is spoken aloud and with the correct emphasis.

Before you say these sentences, predict which of these words are stressed, and then check with your teacher to see if you were right.

Useful language: Summarising a discussion

Summing up your position

We finally all agreed that ... ③

After much consideration, we decided that ... ③

All things considered, we felt that ... ④

On balance, we felt that ... ②

We couldn't reach agreement on this issue ... ③

Some of us felt that ..., whilst others ... ④

Recognising strong arguments against your position

It's true that ... ①

We recognised that ... ①

We're fully aware that ... ②

One has to acknowledge that ... ②

Qualifying your position

This action should only be taken if ... ④

So, although we agreed with the statement, we stressed that ... ⑤

4.5 ⊕ Listen to the recording of a student using the phrases. Practise saying them in a way that is natural.

4.6 Prepare to summarise the outcome of your discussion of one of the statements from Task 3.1 for the whole class. Try to use the *Useful language* in your summary.

4.7 Listen to the summaries given by the other groups. Do you have any comments or questions for them?

Seminar Skills: It is often better to appoint a chairperson in a discussion involving many different people. This will help the management of the discussion. Task 5 looks at the role of the chairperson.

Task 5: Online learning

5.1 Online learning is rapidly becoming more popular as an increasing number of students choose to study in this way. Make some notes in the box on the opposite page about the advantages and disadvantages of this kind of learning.

Advantages	Disadvantages
	− not all people have access to the technology

5.2 Now read the two short articles on the topic on pages 77 to 79. Do they provide you with any more ideas?

5.3 You are now going to participate in a discussion on the following topic.

> Online learning will eventually replace many forms of face-to-face teaching.

Think about the points you want to make and what your overall opinion on the issue is.

The chairperson
One of your group will be the chairperson, who will manage the discussion. The chairperson will ensure that the discussion runs smoothly and will sum up the discussion at the end. The role of the chairperson is to keep the discussion going, not to control or dominate it.

Note: Each person should try to make at least one contribution to the discussion. You do not need to wait for the chairperson to invite you to speak. Remember the characteristics of a good seminar participant from Task 1.1.

You will have ten to 15 minutes for this discussion.

The role of chairperson includes the following responsibilities:

- getting the discussion started;
- giving a brief overview of the topic (introducing it);
- possibly giving definitions;
- keeping the discussion going by encouraging everyone to participate;
- clarifying what people say, if necessary;
- ensuring that one person does not dominate;
- checking that all contributions were understood;
- managing the time;
- summing up the discussion at the end.

Useful language: Chairing a discussion

Getting started

Shall we begin?

Today, we're looking at the following question/topic …

Who would like to begin?

Clarification

So what you mean is …

If I've understood you correctly, …

Managing contributions

Thanks, Pete, for your contribution …

OK, Pete, would anyone else like to comment?

Concluding

So, to sum up, …

We're running out of time, so …

Does anyone want to make a final point?

Have I forgotten anything?

Reviewing your participation
To make progress with your speaking, you need to reflect on your performance in speaking activities. This will help you to identify areas for improvement.

5.4 Fill in the Discussion review form in Appendix 8b relating to the discussion you have just had on online learning. After completing it, join with a student from one of the other groups to compare and discuss your responses. If you were a chairperson in the discussion, join with another chairperson.

Make another entry in your learner diary.

Learner diary

Reflect on the characteristics of a good/poor discussion participant given at the start of this unit.

- Do you feel that you were a 'good participant' in the discussion activities in this unit? Can you say why or why not?
- What areas do you think you need to improve on to become a better participant?

If you want, you can make a recording of your thoughts and give it to your teacher to listen to.

R Review: Units 1 and 2

Key skills

Task 1

Work with a partner.

a) What are your top five tips for giving an effective presentation?

b) What are your top five tips for participating effectively in a seminar?

c) What are five of the responsibilities of a chairperson in a discussion?

Useful language

Task 2

Look back at the expressions for agreeing and disagreeing in Unit 1 Task 3.

Work with a partner.

Student A: Read the statements below to Student B.

Student B: Reply with one of the phrases for agreeing and disagreeing. Support your opinion with a reason.

- It is not important if you make grammatical mistakes while you are speaking.
- All students need to improve their study skills before they start a university course.
- The best way to encourage children to learn is through regular tests and exams.
- It is possible to learn a foreign language using a computer.

Student B: Read the statements below to Student A.

Student A: Reply with one of the phrases for agreeing and disagreeing. Support your opinion with a reason.

- Talking to my classmates will not help to improve my English.
- The skill which will help you most at university is being a quick reader.
- No one should leave school before they are 18.
- In 50 years' time, teachers will disappear as computers take their place.

Look at the statements below. The underlined words are not in the correct order. Rearrange the words to form the correct expressions for summing up a discussion.

that much we consideration decided after there are more effective ways of maintaining discipline than through corporal punishment.

considered we things that all felt parents should not be allowed to educate children at home under normal circumstances.

on reach this we agreement couldn't issue. Some of us felt that disruptive children should be taught separately by special teachers, whilst others felt this would destroy their education completely.

we we with although the so stressed agreed statement that it should only be used in extreme situations, when all other possibilities have been tried.

Vocabulary

Check that you remember the meaning (as used in Units 1 and 2) of the words in the box below.

controversial (adj)	to submit (v) an essay	peer (n)	perspective (n)
a participant (n)	to dominate (v)	discipline (n)	to participate (v)

3 Changing roles in the family

In this unit you will:
- develop awareness of how to help your audience follow a presentation;
- present an article to the class, using the language of presentations;
- consider the importance of anticipating arguments before a discussion;
- practise presenting opinions and counter-arguments in a discussion.

Examining underlying assumptions

You may find that other students from different backgrounds have completely different assumptions from you about the world or society or what is natural. Your assumptions may be challenged. This is an opportunity to encounter different world views and perhaps to question your own underlying assumptions about society. The process of questioning and self-questioning is an important part of academic study and development.

Task 1: The meaning of 'family'

1.1 Consider one word which may mean different things to different people: *family*. What are your responses to the following questions?

  a) What is a typical family for you?

  b) In a family, what should the mother provide?

  c) In a family, what should the father provide?

  d) The ideal age to start a family is …

  e) What does the word 'family' mean to you (e.g., *security, conflict*)?

1.2 Compare your ideas in small groups.

Task 2: Aspects of family life

Look at the questions below. What is the situation in your country and why? Is it changing? What do you think the reasons are for any changes? Discuss these points in small groups.

a) What is the average age for people to get married?

b) Is divorce common?

c) If a couple gets divorced, which parent do the children usually stay with?

d) Is it common for people to live alone?

e) What is the average age for a woman to have her first child?

f) What is the average size of a nuclear family?

g) Is birth outside marriage common?

h) Are one-parent families common?

i) Do many people adopt children?

j) How do parents discipline their children?

k) Do parents put their children in nurseries or leave their children with childminders?

> **Presentation Skills:** When you give a presentation, you need to remember your audience and make it easy for them to follow your talk. Tasks 3 and 4 help you to help your audience by looking at different presentation mini-skills. You will practise these skills later by presenting key ideas from an article.

Task 3: Presenting an article (1)

3.1 Read the article on page 80 entitled *Men want to be househusbands*.

3.2 Look at the two OHTs in Appendix 2. One of them is a useful visual aid to support an oral summary of the article, and one is not.

a) Decide which one is a useful visual aid, and which is not. Give reasons for your decision.

b) Now, in groups, make a list of the characteristics of what makes a good visual aid.

3.3 ⓟ Listen to a student presenting key points from the same article. Refer to OHT 2 as you listen. Notice how the presenter expands on the points on the OHT.

3.4 When referring to a text, it is important to separate your own views from the writer's and to indicate clearly to the audience when you give your own views.

Look at the three extracts from the presentation. In which one does the presenter give his own views on the information in the article?

Extract 1

"The article also gives statistics from a magazine survey of 2,000 couples. As you can see, only one-third of those asked, 34 per cent in fact, wanted to continue working full-time after having children. The majority either wanted to return to part-time work or become full-time househusbands."

Extract 2

"The article then goes on to say that the social stigma attached to men stopping work to bring up a family is disappearing … social stigma – this means something people might be ashamed of doing, that society would not approve of. As I said, this is disappearing, so you now see more men coming to schools and playgroups to collect their children."

Extract 3

"So, the article reports on some interesting changes in social attitudes to work and fatherhood. However, it doesn't mention the effect of socioeconomic background on men's decisions or wishes regarding work and parenthood. I mean, the men who are choosing or wanting to give up work to become house-husbands, are these men from high, middle or lower income groups?"

3.5 🎧 Now listen to these three extracts.

a) Underline where the speaker:
- slows down;
- stresses particular words or phrases.

b) Why do you think the speaker does this?

Presentation Skills: When you give your own presentations, you need to make sure you slow down for key pieces of information so that your audience has time to understand what you are saying.

It is also essential that your audience understands the key words of your presentation. It is a good idea to ensure these are on your OHT or slide and are appropriately stressed/defined in your presentation.

3.6 Look again at the full transcript on pages 101 and 102. Find and highlight at least eight of the phrases the presenter uses to refer directly to the article. Write the phrases in the box on page 28.

For example:

As the title suggests, this article deals with an apparent change in the role men would like to play in family life.

Useful language: Referring to an article

1   *this article deals with …*

Task 4: Presenting an article (2)

Summarising the main points in a presentation can be quite challenging. Sometimes it is hard to know what to omit. Imagine you are telling your friend about a film you saw. You do not tell all the details, only the main points. Similarly, when summarising an article, the most important thing is to identify the key information.

4.1   You are going to read the text your teacher recommends and summarise the main ideas in a short presentation. Pick out the main points which you think are important to understanding the article. Try not to have more than four or five points.

To do this, it is essential that you fully understand the article. If you do not understand it after checking the words or using a dictionary, check with one of your classmates – pooling ideas can often lead to a better understanding. You should not try to summarise the article if you do not understand it.

You will prepare the presentation in pairs or small groups. You need to decide who will give the presentation or how you will divide up the presentation within your group. You will have five minutes to present, with two minutes for questions.

Presentation Skills: Presenting information from a text

- Read the text and identify the main ideas and/or key statistics. (If your text has a lot of facts and statistics, you need to select the ones you think are significant.)
- Identify your topic clearly in your opening and give an overview of the text.
- Select carefully what to put on your visual aid. (*Do not* simply write out sections of the text.)
- Try to express the ideas and information in your own words. (*Do not* simply read out or memorise and repeat sections of the text.)
- Distinguish between the information and ideas given in the article and your own views.
- Check the pronunciation of key words, especially those you use most frequently.
- Explain the meaning of difficult or technical words. (Remember: if you have to check the meaning of a word, then your audience may not understand it either.)
- Pause and give the audience time to understand complex information.

4.2 Practise your presentation in your groups. Remember the points from Task 4.1. Give your group's presenter feedback (e.g.,"You need to slow down and pause at that point. The information is complex.", "You should explain the meaning of that word.").

4.3 Present your summary of the article to the class.

    a) As you listen to each presentation, one person in each group should also complete the Presentation assessment form in Appendix 8c. Your teacher will give you copies. The comments you write – suggestions for improvement – are very important, as they will help the speaker for the next time.

    b) After listening to each presentation, in your groups you will have to:

      ● check that you have all understood the main points;

      ● check any points which you were unsure of;

      ● make a note of any questions or comments you would like to make to the presenters.

(Note: you may want to ask the presenter to clarify or repeat something you did not understand.)

4.4 After you have listened to all the presentations, decide which was the most interesting article.

If you completed an assessment form, you should now give this to the presenter.

> **Seminar Skills:** When preparing for a seminar or discussion, it is important to consider issues from opposing sides. This will help you to clarify your thinking and formulate your opinions on a topic. Considering an opposing position to your own can help you to strengthen your own position. On the other hand, you may find that you start to qualify or modify, or even change your own position. In Task 5 you will practise these skills.

Task 5: Arguments and counter-arguments in seminar discussions

5.1 Look at the following statement.

> Women are naturally more suited to childcare than men.

You will discuss this statement in groups of four. Two of you will support this view. The other two will oppose this view. Before you begin, you need to prepare your arguments with your partner.

● What will your main points be?

● What do you think the other pair's main points will be?

● How will you counter their arguments?

5.2 Now debate the statement in groups of four. The pair who support the statement should begin by presenting their main points. The opposing pair should then counter these points and present their own points.

5.3 Reflect on your participation in the discussion.

- Did you state your opinion clearly?
- Did you anticipate the arguments of the other pair and counter them?

5.4 ⊕ Listen to the recording of students exchanging opinions on different topics. Look at the expressions below which the speakers use to exchange opinions. Tick the expressions you hear.

Useful language: Exchanging opinions

Asking for opinions

☐ *What are your views on this issue?*

☐ *Do you agree?*

Presenting your own opinion

☐ *Well, I think …*

☐ *It seems to me that …*

☐ *In my view, …*

Countering the other person's opinion

☐ *I take your point, but …*

☐ *I understand what you're saying, but …*

☐ *Well, I'm not sure if that's quite true …*

☐ *But surely …*

5.5 Change partners and prepare to debate one of the following statements. Decide which pair will support the view given and which pair will oppose it.

Statements

It is better to wait until you are older to start a family.

Living on your own has more advantages than disadvantages.

Wealth will not bring you happiness.

Prepare for your discussion as in Task 5.1.

This time you should try to use some of the expressions from the *Useful language* box in Task 5.4.

Learner diary

Do you feel more confident presenting in front of an audience?

- How did this unit help you?
- What do you feel you still need to do to improve your presentation skills?

Do you feel more confident participating in discussions?

- How did this unit help you?
- What do you feel you still need to do to be a better participant in seminar discussions?

Developing your presentation skills

If you want further guidelines on developing your presentation skills, look at Appendix 3.

4

A healthy lifestyle

In this unit you will:
- use a text to support or modify your ideas;
- practise active listening;
- develop strategies to check your understanding as a listener;
- exchange information effectively by anticipating your listener's difficulties.

Reading into speaking

When preparing for a seminar, you will often need to refer to reading texts on the topic in order to develop your ideas further. You will probably have your own ideas on the topic before you start reading. As you read, you may find support for your ideas. However, you may find that you change or adjust your views as you read. This may in turn influence the ideas you present in the seminar. The ability to integrate and develop ideas from your reading is an essential part of academic life.

Task 1: Questionnaire

1.1   Complete the questionnaire below.

How healthy is your lifestyle?

a)   How often do you do exercise?

b)   How many hours a day do you spend sitting?

c)   How regular are your meals?

d)   How much fruit and vegetables do you eat?

e)   Do you prepare your own food or do you eat processed food?

f)   How often do you eat junk food?

g)   Do you take vitamin supplements?

h)   How many times a year do you have a cold?

i)   Are you a smoker?

1.2   Use the questions to interview your partner. Do you think your partner has a healthy lifestyle?

Task 2: Who is responsible?

Nowadays there is often discussion about who is responsible for various aspects of life. Is it the individual or the government? For example, recently the governments in some countries have introduced a ban on smoking in all public places. In other countries, individuals can decide whether or not they wish to smoke in a public place.

2.1 What is the situation in your country?

    a) Read the following statements. Do you agree or disagree with each one? Give a reason for your answer.

    b) In small groups, discuss each point briefly.

It is the responsibility of the individual to give up smoking.

It is the responsibility of employers to reduce stress levels among their staff.

2.2 Who else might be responsible for the problems mentioned?

2.3 Did you agree or disagree with the other people in your group?

> **Seminar Skills:** You need to spend time preparing for a seminar. What do you think about the topic? Does any of the reading you do influence what you think? How will you express what you want to say? Task 3 asks you to prepare for a discussion.

Task 3: Preparation for a discussion

3.1 Do you think the following statement is true or false? Give your reasons.

It is the responsibility of individuals themselves to avoid becoming obese by ensuring they have a balanced diet and a healthy lifestyle.

Can you give reasons for your opinion? Discuss this with your partner.

When you have finished, write down your opinion in the middle of a blank piece of paper (maximum three lines).

3.2 Read the article on page 92.

    a) Is there anything in it which supports your view?

    b) Is there anything in it which might make you modify or change your opinion?

    c) Does it provide you with extra ideas?

3.3 When you have read the article, write down relevant points around your original opinion on your piece of paper. Add points which either develop, change or support your view.

See the example below.

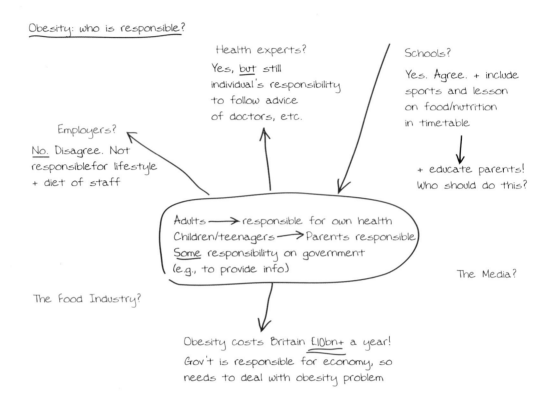

Obesity: who is responsible?

Health experts?
Yes, but still individual's responsibility to follow advice of doctors, etc.

Schools?
Yes. Agree. + include sports and lesson on food/nutrition in time-table

Employers?
No. Disagree. Not responsible for lifestyle + diet of staff

+ educate parents! Who should do this?

Adults ⟶ responsible for own health
Children/teenagers ⟶ Parents responsible
Some responsibility on government (e.g., to provide info)

The Media?

The Food Industry?

Obesity costs Britain £10bn+ a year! Gov't is responsible for economy, so needs to deal with obesity problem

Blue = original opinion; red = notes from text; black = additional notes, after reading text

3.4 You are going to discuss the statement in Task 3.1 in groups of four or five.

a) Prepare what you are going to say. You may refer to your notes and the article, if you wish.

b) Now discuss the topic in groups.

3.5 Summarise the outcome of your discussion for the class. Did your group agree or disagree with the statement overall?

Seminar Skills: Discussions are interactive. You do not just present your own views. You listen and react to what other people are saying. Task 4 looks at this aspect of seminars. After you have looked at and practised appropriate language expressions, Task 4.5 requires you to put these skills and language into practice in a seminar situation.

Task 4: Being an active listener

Listening is an important aspect of participating in a discussion. You need to listen because your ideas may be influenced by what other students say. An important aspect of listening actively is checking that you have understood correctly and showing when you do not understand. As a speaker, you also need to make sure that people have understood you.

4.1   Consider your role as a listener and speaker in the discussion you had on obesity. Think about the two questions below, and discuss these with your group.

a)   As a listener, did you interrupt the speaker at any point if you did not understand something?

b)   As a speaker, did you check that your listeners were following you?

4.2   The *Useful language* box shows a number of expressions you can use.
Listen to the recording of these expressions in context. Tick the ones which you hear.

Useful language:
Clarifying and confirming understanding

Confirming understanding as a listener

- [ ]   *So what you're saying is …*

- [ ]   *So in your view, …*

- [ ]   *If I understand you correctly, you're saying …*

Checking understanding as a speaker

- [ ]   *Do you understand what I mean?*

- [ ]   *Do you follow what I am saying?*

- [ ]   *Am I making sense?*

Showing that you do not understand

- [ ]   *I'm not sure I understand what you mean.*

- [ ]   *I didn't quite follow you. Could you explain that point again, please?*

- [ ]   *Could you repeat that, please?*

4.3   Now practise listening actively and checking understanding. Look at the two statements below.

Statement 1

Free health care should not be given to smokers.

Statement 2

Advertising of junk food should be banned.

Student A: Decide whether you agree or disagree with Statement 1 and give the main reason for your view. Give your opinion and a supporting reason to Student B. Check that he or she understands your points, using one of the phrases for checking understanding in the box in Task 4.2.

Student B: Confirm your understanding of A's opinion by summarising what he or she says. Use one of the phrases for confirming understanding from the box in Task 4.2.

Now change roles and discuss Statement 2.

4.4 Now go back to your points on obesity. You are going to discuss this statement again, but with different people. This time, make sure that you use the interactive strategies that you have just practised.

4.5 Complete the Discussion review form in Appendix 8d. Compare what you wrote with the other members of your group.

> **Seminar Skills:** Relating information from a text to someone who has not read it is an aspect of academic life. You need to inform your listener and make sure they have understood the main points. It is unhelpful to exchange information without checking understanding. Task 5 deals with exchanging information in a cooperative way.

Task 5: Comparing information

5.1 Answer the questions below on the topic of stress.

a) What are the main causes of stress?

b) How does stress affect your health?

c) Can stress ever be good for you?

d) What are some ways of dealing with stress?

Compare your answers in pairs.

5.2 Your teacher will give you one of two articles on the topic of stress to read for homework. Later, you are going to exchange information on this. To do this successfully, you will need to:

- ensure that you fully understand the information;
- anticipate what difficulties your listener will have;
- use some of the strategies from Task 4.

Complete the column in the table in Task 5.3 with the information from your text. Select what information to include. You do not need to include all the points given. Check the meaning of any difficult words that are relevant to the task. Do not simply complete the column without understanding. Check your completed column with people who have read the same text as you.

5.3 Now sit with someone who read the other text. Exchange information and complete the column relating to the other text. Use your notes from the column you filled in – do not look at the original text.

Make sure your partner understands you and you fully understand what your partner says as you complete the table. This means you should:

- check the pronunciation of any difficult words before you start;
- check your partner has understood what you say;

ask your partner to repeat or explain if you do not understand;

remember to use the language expressions for checking understanding as a speaker and as a listener from Task 4.2.

	Article A: Stress: To what extent can it be controlled?	Article B: Stress: Keeping things in perspective
Definition of stress		
Examples of symptoms of stress		
Suggestions for dealing with stress		

5.4 What similarities and differences did you find between the information given in the two articles?

5.5 Did you check that your partner understood what you said? Did you ask your partner to help if you did not understand?

5.6 If you were having a discussion on the following topic, what information from your articles would you use? Decide quickly in groups of three or four.

"Relaxation techniques are the best method for dealing with stress."

Learner diary

Reflect on your participation in the discussions in this unit.

- How easy do you find it to follow discussions and make relevant contributions?

- What problems do you have with this?

- Can you think of ways to help you improve your participation?

- In discussions and presentations, how can you help people to follow what you are saying?

R Review: Units 3 and 4

Key skills

Task 1

Work with a partner.

a) What are your five top tips for presenting the content of an article?

b) What criteria should you use when assessing a presentation?

c) Give reasons why it is important to listen actively in a discussion.

Task 2

a) What are 'underlying assumptions'?

b) Why is it important to support your ideas in academic discussions and written work?

Useful language

Task 3

Look at the *Useful language* box in Unit 4 Task 4.2.

Work in pairs.

Student A: Look at the statements below and give your opinion plus a supporting reason for each one. Check Student B understands.

Student B: Listen to Student A's opinion. Confirm you understand (or show you don't understand).

Statements:

Men and women are equally good at childcare.

Older parents make better parents.

It is the government's responsibility to keep people healthy.

Now look at the *Useful language* box in Unit 3 Task 5.4.

Student B: Look at the statements below and give your opinion and a supporting reason for each one. Ask for Student A's opinion.

Student A: Listen to Student B's opinion. Respond with your own opinion.

Statements

A women's role in society should be to have children and look after the home.

A society with a higher standard of living has higher levels of happiness.

If you feel stressed as a student, you should give up your course.

Vocabulary

Task 4

Check with your partner that you remember the meaning of the words below.

Now fill in the missing columns of word forms.

Noun	Verb	Adjective
	to challenge	
assumption		
		underlying
		complex
responsibility		

Choose three words from the table and put them into sentences which show you understand their meaning.

5 The influence of the media

In this unit you will:
- practise describing charts and data;
- practise seminar skills by building on what previous speakers have said;
- identify and practise using phrases to refer to other speakers.

The use of data

Data is a key part of academic study. Charts, graphs and tables are often included in both written work and presentations. They are used as evidence, to support the points the writer or speaker is trying to make.

Task 1: Matching definitions

In the left-hand column below are 11 words and phrases commonly used for kinds of TV or radio programmes. Match each word with the appropriate definition in the right-hand column.

a) soap opera

i) A programme in which the public takes part by phoning in with comments.

b) quiz show

ii) A long-running drama of the day-to-day experience of a community of characters.

c) reality TV

iii) A programme in which contestants try to score points by answering questions correctly.

d) chat show

iv) An informative, in-depth examination of a fairly serious topic.

e) sitcom

v) A programme in which contestants take part in various games to win prizes.

f) documentary

vi) An adaptation of a major work of literature.

g) phone-in

vii) A programme in which a presenter asks a celebrity to talk about him/herself.

h) classic drama

viii) A team of experts redecorate your house or redesign your garden or change your image.

i) makeover programme

ix) A programme in which a group of people from the public live together for a period of time, observed by camera 24 hours a day, and are voted off.

j) game show

x) A comedy of character and situation involving the same characters in each episode.

k) miniseries

xi) A programme which has several episodes with the same characters.

Task 2: Discussion

2.1 Discuss in groups.

a) Which kind of programme is most popular in your country?

b) What kind of audience does each of these kinds of programme appeal to?

c) Why are reality TV programmes so popular?

d) Which kind of programme do you watch most often in your own country?

e) Which kind do you least enjoy?

f) Which kinds have you seen examples of on English-language television, if any?

2.2 Think of a particular programme (in your country or the country where you are studying) that you especially enjoyed or disliked in the last year or so. Briefly describe the programme and explain your reaction to it.

> **Presentation Skills:** When giving a presentation, you may have to refer to charts and graphs to support your point. It is important to guide your audience to the main points of the data or those points which are relevant to the argument you are presenting. See Task 3.

Task 3: Presenting information

3.1 Look at the graph here. It shows the results of a survey of the changing patterns of people going to the cinema, according to age range. What trends does it show? Discuss with a partner.

3.2 ⏵ Listen to the description of the data shown. What details does the speaker highlight? What point is the speaker making by showing this data?

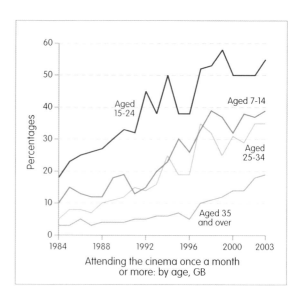

Presenting data

● Briefly outline what the data is about.

● Comment on the features which are relevant and support the points you are making.

3.3 🔊 Listen to the recording again and fill in the gaps in the excerpt.

_____ monthly visits to the cinema by age groups between 1984 and 2003.

_____ , young people aged between 15 and 24 are the most likely age group to go to the cinema. Fifty-four per cent of this age group attended the cinema once a month or more in Great Britain in 2003. In 2003, 39 per cent of children aged seven to 14 went to the cinema once a month or more, _____ . The percentage for both these age groups has risen noticeably since 1984.

_____ going to the cinema is still a popular form of entertainment, despite the arrival of videos, DVDs and computer games.

Useful language: Referring to data

This graph gives information about …

This chart describes …

This chart clearly shows that …

This line here shows …

As these figures illustrate, …

3.4 Data can be used to illustrate certain points. For example, the chart in Task 3.1 was used to illustrate the point that the cinema is still a popular form of entertainment with young people, despite the arrival of videos, DVDs and computer games.

For your next class, find a chart or graph which presents information which interests you. It might be from a newspaper or magazine. What point could you make, using the data as evidence? Be prepared to make a point and use the chart to support your point. Select relevant pieces of information from the chart or graph to describe.

Task 4: Listening

4.1 🔊 You are going to hear a journalist talking about the BBC. Read the questions below before you listen.

a) What were the three purposes of the BBC when it was originally set up?

b) In what ways did John Reith, the first director general of the BBC, believe that the BBC should be independent?

c) In the 1920s, what caused conflict between the BBC and the government?

d) More recently, what was the main area of conflict between the government and the BBC?

e) How does the BBC finance itself?

4.2 Read the transcript on pages 104 to 106 to check your answers.

4.3 The journalist comments that "the BBC is still the most trusted organisation in the country." To what extent do you agree that television coverage of news events can be trusted?

Seminar Skills: In the last unit, you looked at the skill of active listening. This is important because your contributions to the discussion need to relate to what has been said previously. You may need to show this by referring to previous speakers. This helps the discussion to develop a sense of direction.

In addition, you may find that your ideas develop and change as you interact with other students. You might have a clearer idea of what you think or what your position is by the end of a seminar. Task 5 looks at this aspect of seminars.

Task 5: Building on what the previous speaker has said

5.1 Discuss the following questions with a partner.

a) What does "freedom of speech" mean to you?

b) Are there any negative aspects of freedom of speech?

5.2 Look at the statements below. Decide if you agree or disagree with each one, and why.

a) Freedom of speech is absolutely necessary in a democracy.

b) There should be no limits on freedom of speech.

c) Complete freedom of speech may mean that some individuals may feel unsafe in a society.

d) The government needs to limit freedom of speech to protect minority groups.

5.3 ⊙ Listen to three students discussing freedom of speech.

The two women state that there should be no limit on freedom of speech. What does the man believe? What are his reasons? Does he change his opinion?

5.4 Look at the transcript on pages 106 and 107. Underline the phrases which the speakers use to refer to the comments of other speakers.

For example:

When you say "an absolute principle", do you mean that anyone can say or broadcast or print anything they want …

Write the phrases in the *Useful language* box opposite.

Useful language: Referring to other speakers

Task 6: Group discussion

6.1 You are now going to have a discussion on one of the following topics related to the media. Your group can decide which of these topics to choose.

a) Media independence from the government is essential.

b) There should be censorship in the media.

c) TV has a negative impact on children/family life.

d) The media controls the information which the public receives, so whoever controls the media controls what the public think.

6.2 When you have chosen your topic, spend five minutes making notes on the points you want to make. You can refer to any of the ideas in Tasks 4 and 5.

6.3 Now discuss your chosen topic. Remember to listen carefully to what other students say, as this may help you to develop your ideas.

Try to use at least two of the phrases from Task 5.4 for referring to other speakers.

6.4 Fill in the Discussion review form in Appendix 8e.

Task 7: Over to you

For the next session, you need to find a recent article from an English-language media source which reports on the news or events in your country. This could be from a newspaper or magazine or from the Web. A good source is to go to the website of a newspaper (e.g., www.guardian.co.uk) or broadcaster (e.g., www.bbc.co.uk) and do an 'Archive Search'.

a) **What** events or issues does the article report on? You will need to summarise the main points. (See the *Useful language* box in Unit 3 Task 3.6.)

b) **How** does the article report on the events? Do you think there is any bias in the reporting, or does it seem to be objective? Do you think it might mislead readers in any way about your country? Do you think this information was reported on in a similar way in the media in your own country?

Bring a copy of the article to the next session. Be prepared to report back on points a) and b). You will have two minutes.

Learner diary

- On your future courses, what sort of data do you anticipate you will be dealing with?

- Do you feel more confident in describing data orally? If not, what do you feel you need to practise more?

- Has your participation in group discussion changed since the beginning of the course? In what ways?

- What aspects of participation in group discussion do you still find difficult?

6 Consolidation unit

In the past five units, you have worked on the following skills:
- presenting your point of view and looking at different perspectives;
- presenting, agreeing with and countering an argument;
- building on what previous speakers have said;
- taking the role of chairperson;
- using appropriate language phrases.

1 Seminar skills

You will now have the opportunity to further practise these skills by leading a seminar discussion. Leading a seminar discussion means that you are responsible for the initial input, as well as summing up at the end. This is different from chairing a discussion, where you are only responsible for ensuring the discussion goes smoothly. Every student will have the opportunity to lead a seminar discussion.

2 Choosing the topic

Choose a controversial subject; it needs to be a subject of interest to the people in your group/class, and a topic which they will be able to discuss.

Prepare an overview of the topic. This should be a summary of the main issues, as well as a list of discussion points for the group to consider. Or you might like to present some points on both sides of the issue, before opening it up to discussion by all the participants.

For some ideas on seminar topics, see Appendix 4.

3 During the discussion

You will be leading the discussion for the whole group.

You have 20 minutes for the discussion, including the time for presenting the topic and summing up the discussion at the end. You should only take three or four minutes at most to outline your ideas before the discussion begins.

Make sure that everyone has the opportunity to participate and that it is not left to one or two students to dominate.

If there is a silence, you will need to build on what has been said before, or ask a question or invite someone to contribute, in order to keep the discussion going.

Allow about two minutes at the end to sum up.

4 Model demonstration

Your teacher will give you a model demonstration in which you will participate. Remember the characteristics of being a good seminar participant discussed in Unit 2.

5 Presentation skills

So far in the course, you have worked on developing the following aspects of presentation skills.

- planning a presentation;
- selecting and organising your ideas;
- introducing a topic;
- delivering a presentation clearly;
- using visual aids;
- using signpost expressions to guide the listener.

The introduction to your seminar discussion is like a mini-presentation, so you should put these skills into practice.

6 Useful language

You should review the *Useful language* boxes from each unit and try to use the language where appropriate.

Learner diary

After you have led a seminar, reflect on the experience in your diary.

- How did you feel immediately afterwards?
- What aspects did you feel satisfied with?
- What aspects of managing a seminar do you feel you need to work on?

Use the assessment form in Appendix 8f to give feedback to the seminar leader. Your teacher will provide you with copies.

R Review: Units 5 and 6

Key skills

Task 1

Work with a partner.

a) How should you begin when reporting on any information or data?

b) What are the key factors which make a seminar discussion successful?

c) What do you find easiest about participation in a seminar? What do you find most difficult?

d) Think of an article you have read recently – it might be an academic article or one from a newspaper. In one sentence, summarise it for your partner.

Useful language

Task 2

Look at the table here, which gives information based on a survey of 1,000 students, asking them how they spent their time on Saturday evenings. With a partner, identify the most important information and decide on three points you might present.

Make sure you use some of these language expressions.

- This table gives information about …
- This table clearly shows …
- From the table, it is clear that …
- As these figures illustrate, …

What other information would you like to have about the survey which the table does not show?

Table 1: Students' social activities on Saturday evenings

Part-time jobs	19%
Going clubbing	45%
Doing sports	7%
Shopping	9%
Speaking extensively in English	38%
In the pub	51%

Vocabulary

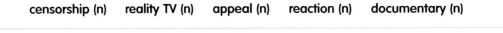

Task 4

Check that you know the meaning of the words below, then fill in the gaps with the appropriate word from the list. One word is not used.

> censorship (n)   reality TV (n)   appeal (n)   reaction (n)   documentary (n)

a) If the BBC shows a programme which the public feels is not appropriate, there is often a strong _____ from the public.

b) Part of the _____ of TV is that it is an easy option; you can just sit and watch and no effort is required.

c) _____ in the media is very important in order to protect vulnerable people.

d) Currently, _____ is popular, where a group of people from the public, often well-known people, live together under camera scrutiny 24 hours a day, and are voted off.

7 The world of work

In this unit you will:

    prepare for a discussion by thinking through the issues beforehand;

    use a listening source to support your viewpoint;

    consider strategies for entering into a discussion;

    research and plan a presentation.

Supporting your point of view

In academic study, including when you prepare for a seminar, you will often have to refer to a variety of written and spoken resources. You can use these to give evidence to support your viewpoint, whether or not you agree with the viewpoint expressed in an article. However, before you consult these sources, it is useful to spend some time thinking about the topic and working out your opinion on the basis of what you already know. Your position may subsequently change as you engage with the texts and the views of other students.

Task 1: Your attitude to work

1.1   After you graduate, you will probably be looking for work or returning to work. How important are the following aspects of work to you?

    a)   Tick the boxes, where 5 means *very important* and 1 means *less important*.

    b)   What aspect of work would you add to the remaining three boxes – factors which are important to you personally, but are not included?

    c)   Compare and discuss your responses in pairs.

	1	2	3	4	5
The amount I earn					
The people I work with					
The amount of responsibility I have					
The variety of tasks I do					
The degree of challenge I have					
The job security I have					
The possibilities I have of promotion					
The number of hours I work					
The possibility of working flexible hours					

1.2 Careers advice services often make use of questionnaires to help direct people towards a suitable career. See Appendix 5 for an example of such a questionnaire.

a) Complete the questionnaire for homework. You will need to bring the completed questionnaire to class. In the next lesson your teacher will give you the key so you can analyse the results.

b) In the next lesson you should compare your results in groups. Comment on the analysis – to what extent do you agree with it?

Task 2: Finding a job in your country

Discuss the following points in pairs or small groups.

a) How easy is it for graduates to find work in your country at the moment?

b) What sort of information do job applicants usually provide to employers on curriculum vitae?

c) What is most important when finding a job in your country:

the reputation of the university you attended?

the qualification you obtained (undergraduate degree, postgraduate degree)?

the result you obtained?

the people you know?

other factors?

Task 3: Gender at work

Look at the table below, which compares women in the UK workforce in 1975 and 2006. Answer these questions.

a) What do you think are the most significant trends in the table?

b) How does men's pay compare with women's?

c) Do women have similar opportunities as men to rise to senior positions?

d) How does this trend compare with the pattern in your country?

Table 7.1: Women at work in the UK in 1975 and 2006

	1975	2006
Women in employment	9.1 million	12.5 million
Full-time gender pay gap	29%	17.1%
Part-time gender pay gap	42%	38.4%
Working mothers	47%	66%
Working mothers with pre-school children	25%	52%
Mothers back at work eight months after giving birth	15%	70%
Female managers	1.8%	33.1%
Female directors	0.6%	14.4%

Source: Equal Opportunities Commission - *Guardian* 14/01/06

Task 4: Equal opportunities

4.1   You are going to discuss the following topic:

> There should be equal opportunities for men and women to do any job.

4.2   First you should discuss the questions below with a partner.

a)   Are some jobs more appropriate for men than women? Give examples and say why.

b)   Are some jobs more appropriate for women than men? Give examples and say why.

c)   To what extent does nature or nurture influence the jobs men and women choose to do?

4.3   You are going to listen to an interview with Sonia Gurjao, the author of a research paper entitled 'Inclusivity: the Changing Role of Women in the Construction Workforce'.

Before you listen, read the following extract from the paper's introduction:

> The UK's construction industry is facing a skills shortage that is a threat to the long-term health of the industry. It is suffering recruitment problems with its traditional source of labour – young men aged 16-19. Efforts are being made to recruit women into the workforce, but with limited success. In the short term, the industry is filling the skills gap using workers from low-wage economies. What is needed is a skilled workforce that sees its long-term future in the UK construction industry. To meet the challenge of the skills gap, the recruitment of women is no longer simply a nice thing to do; it has become a necessity.
>
> Women in the UK construction industry currently account for under ten per cent of the workforce, reflecting their under-representation in an industry that fails to attract and retain women.

4.4   Now read the questions which the interviewer asks Sonia.

a)   What are the reasons why more women today are participating in the labour market?

b)   Is the construction industry a common career choice for women?

c)   Why does the construction industry need more women to join it?

d)   Has the construction industry made any attempts to recruit women into the industry?

e)   The construction industry has a problem with keeping the women who join it. Why is that and is there a solution to the problem?

f)   What are the main barriers which women face today in joining or staying in the construction industry?

4.5 🎧 Listen to the interview.

a) Take notes of Sonia's replies to the questions.

b) Is there any information from the interview you might be able to use in your discussion?

4.6 You should now discuss the seminar topic in groups. You may appoint a chairperson to manage the discussion.

Task 5: Taking your turn

Think back to the discussion you have just had on gender at work.

a) Do any of the statements match what you felt about your role in the discussion (or in discussions generally)?

> You had problems entering the discussion, even though you had something important to say.

> You wanted to speak, but did not have the opportunity because:

> – the discussion moved too quickly and you missed a chance to speak at a relevant point.

> – other people wanted to speak at the same time as you.

> – you did not want to interrupt or speak over other people.

b) What strategies or language do you think you could use to make your points in these situations?

In addition, you may find that discussions between many people are often not very "tidy", because people may respond to different points at different times.

On the following page is *Useful language* to help you take your turn in the situations outlined.

Useful language: Taking your turn

You want to make a point that is relevant at this moment in the discussion. You need to enter the discussion politely, but firmly:

Can I just come in here?

You want to make a point, but the discussion moves on before you can contribute or finish. You can still make your point later:

To go back to my earlier point, …

Coming back to what John said earlier, …

I think I agree with the point you made earlier, Anne.

You start speaking at the same moment as another student. Both of you stop to let the other speak. It is polite to offer each other the chance to continue:

A: *Sorry, carry on.*

B: *No, go ahead.*

A: *Thanks. I think …* [A makes his/her point and then invites B to speak] *Sorry, you were going to say …*

B: *Yes, I think …*

You notice that a quiet student is trying to speak, but other students keep speaking first. You can help the quiet student to get the attention of the group:

I think David has been trying to make a point.

David, did you want to make a point?

If you have difficulties taking your turn in the next discussion, try to use some of the strategies and language above.

Presentation Skills: When planning a presentation, you need a topic and you need to find a focus within the topic. You then need to generate ideas around your focus. You also need to organise your ideas, ensuring your main points are relevant to your focus. Task 8 looks at this aspect of presentations.

Task 6: The changing nature of work in the 21st century

6.1   Check your understanding of the terms and ideas below, related to the topic of work.

teleworking   ethical working practices   the 24/7 society   working flexi-time
the knowledge-based economy   corporate culture
the decline in manufacturing industry   job-sharing   management style

6.2 In small groups, choose one of the topics above related to the theme of "work" and choose one of the questions below to discuss in relation to your chosen topic. This may help you find a focus for your presentation.

a) What are its causes and what are its consequences?

b) Is there a problem associated with it? What are possible solutions to the problem?

c) Can aspects of it be compared and contrasted (e.g., between different cultures)?

d) How has it developed over time? How might it continue to develop?

For example:

Topic: Teleworking

Question: What are its causes and consequences?

Causes:

– technological developments allowing easier communication between workplace and home

– more women wishing to work from home after having children

Can you think of any consequences?

6.3 Either:

a) Report on your ideas from Task 6.2 to the class. The class should listen and respond (ask questions/add ideas).

OR

b) Develop your ideas into a full presentation in your groups. You should carry out some research in your groups by consulting a range of sources. Decide how you will divide up the research and report back on your ideas.

You should refer to your sources in your presentation, incorporating data or quotations where appropriate. These should be acknowledged.

6.4 Give your presentations to the class. Evaluate the other presentations according to the following criteria:

Organisation

Are the main ideas logically ordered?

Are the introduction and conclusion linked to the main ideas?

Content

Are the main ideas relevant to the focus?

Are the ideas developed in sufficient depth?

Learner diary

- Which activity did you enjoy most in this unit?

- Have you moderated any of your views as a result of what you listened to and discussed in the unit?

- Do you prefer to give a presentation where the title is fixed, or do you prefer when you can choose your own title? Please give a reason for your choice.

- What aspects of giving a presentation do you still find difficult?

8 Protecting the environment

In this unit you will:
- design a questionnaire and obtain feedback on it;
- collect and present data;
- participate in a debate;
- give a presentation on a global issue.

Collecting and presenting data

On your academic course, you may be required to collect, analyse and present data. You may have to design the method of data collection yourself. In this unit you are going to choose a topic, design a questionnaire, analyse the results and then present them.

Task 1: Designing a questionnaire

1.1 Imagine that you want to learn about people's attitudes towards the environment. Your overall aim might be to determine how much responsibility people are taking individually to protect and preserve the environment. You should think of this topic in the broadest sense, including issues such as throwing things away when they are still functional.

Below is a list of some of the topics you might ask questions about in your questionnaire.

> **recycling in the home**   **saving energy in the house**   **use of transport**
>
> **shopping for eco-friendly products**   **supporting environmental groups**

When preparing such a questionnaire, you need to:
- decide what the focus of your questionnaire is (e.g., what people do in relation to their home);
- identify eight to ten questions for your topic;
- make sure each question elicits relevant information.

1.2 Sometimes, questions in questionnaires are poorly designed, because they do not elicit the information required, may not be appropriate or do not allow for the subject to give the answer which is true for them.

Look at some examples of poorly designed questions. What is wrong with each one? How could each one be improved?

I	How old are you?
2	Do you use public transport often?
3	Do you recycle:
	– every day?
	– once a week?
	– once a year?
4	Do you like environmentally friendly products?

1.3 In groups of three, prepare eight to ten questions that would be suitable for the questionnaire discussed in Task 1.1.

1.4 Exchange questionnaires with another group. Evaluate their questionnaire.

- Does it elicit the relevant information?
- Are any of the questions poorly designed?
- Have you any suggestions for improvement?

1.5 Choose one of the questions from your questionnaire.

a) Ask all your classmates the same question, making a note of their responses.

b) Report back on your findings to the rest of the class, using the expressions in the *Useful language* box.

Useful language: Expressing quantity

Most		of those interviewed/questioned …	reported/
Nearly all			stated/
Approximately	half	of the subjects …	claimed that …
Approaching	a third	of the respondents …	
Just under	50%		
Just over			

1.6 In groups of three, brainstorm ideas and choose a new topic for your own questionnaire.

You will need to bring three copies of the questionnaire to the next session in order to pilot it with another group.

Task 2: Piloting your questionnaire

2.1 Give your questionnaire to another group to complete.

2.2 When you have filled in the questionnaire you have received from another group, discuss it with your group.

- Are the questions clear?
- Could the questionnaire be improved in any way, e.g., more effective layout?
- Are there any other questions which could be added?

2.3 Return the questionnaire to the group which designed it, and explain any comments you have.

2.4 Revise your own questionnaire in view of the feedback you received from the other group.

Task 3: Administering your questionnaire

You now need to collect data from 15 people, using your questionnaire.

You should interview your subjects face-to-face and note down their answers.
Your pronunciation needs to be clear. Practise asking your questions with someone from another group. Check pronunciation of individual words with your teacher if necessary.

Presentation Skills: Data is often included in presentations, as discussed in Unit 5, to support the points you are making. If you have collected the data yourself, you need to think about how to present the data and what language to use. See the *Useful language* box and Task 4.

Task 4: Reporting back on your findings

4.1 You will need to decide how you are going to present your data, e.g., pie chart, bar graph, table. Your choice will be determined by the kind of information you want to present – what format will allow you to present your information most effectively?

4.2 Listen to a recording of a student using *Useful language* expressions from Task 1. Underline the words or phrases from the box which the speaker uses.

Presentation Skills: You should follow the steps below in your presentation.

- Present data.
- Highlight significant data.
- Discuss the implications of the data.
- Evaluate the design of the questionnaire; how well did it work?

Task 5: Participating in a debate

A debate is a formal forum of discussion. In a debate situation, there are two teams: one in favour of the motion and the other against. There are three people on each team. Two members of the team have to make a speech. The third member of each team should be ready to pick up points made by the opposition and respond. The other team members can help this member by passing on any ideas.

5.1 You will debate the following motion.

> Protection of the environment is mainly dependent on government policies; leaving it to individuals will not work.

5.2 Preparation for a debate.

a) Work with your team to list as many points as possible to support your side, with examples and evidence.

b) Try to think of points which the opposition will raise. Come up with counter-arguments.

c) Decide which team member will make which points.

5.3 Rules of a debate.

- Each person has a limited time to make their speech (your teacher will tell you how long each speaker has).

- The member of the team which proposes the motion (Team 1) starts, followed by a member of the opposition (Team 2) giving their speech, then back to Team 1, until all have spoken.

- The last speaker in each team summarises the discussion, including a rebuttal of what the opposite team has said.

- The discussion is then open to the floor, with any points the audience wishes to make.

- A vote by the "judges" decides the winning team.

> **Presentation Skills:** In the previous unit, you looked at finding a focus for a presentation and the need to develop your ideas around your focus. Task 6 gives further practice in this skill.

Task 6: Perspectives on global issues

6.1 Below is a list of problems related to global issues. Think about the short- and long-term consequences of not dealing with each of these problems. In pairs, discuss why it is important that solutions are found to each one.

- The use of fossil fuels

- Deforestation

- The wealth gap between developed and developing countries

- The spread of cyber-crime

- The spread of infectious diseases

- The disappearance of endangered languages

Make a note in the box on page 62 of consequences for each problem.

Problem	Consequences
The use of fossil fuels	
Deforestation	
The wealth gap between developed and developing nations	
The spread of cyber-crime	
The spread of infectious diseases	
The disappearance of endangered languages	

6.2 In small groups, choose one of the problems listed in Task 6.1 and suggest some practical solutions for dealing with the problem. Do not complete the *Evaluation* column yet.

Topic:	
Possible solutions	Evaluation of solution

6.3 Now look at your solutions and evaluate which are the most effective. This means considering:

- the advantages and disadvantages of each solution;
- what is necessary to make each solution work;
- whether a suggested solution may then create further problems.

a) Add some evaluative comments after each solution in the box in Task 6.2.

b) Try to reach an overall conclusion as to the most effective way or ways of dealing with the problem.

6.4 As a group, take one problem and present it, together with possible solutions and evaluation. Put your key ideas on an OHT.

The audience should try to ask questions at the end of each presentation.

Learner diary

- Did you manage to identify the most important information from your data and present it clearly to your audience?
- What did you learn in the unit about questionnaire design?
- In what way do you think your discussion skills have most improved on this course?
- Think about your role in the debate: what was the most challenging aspect of participation?

Review: Units 7 and 8

Key skills

Task 1

Work with a partner.

a) What five tips would you give anyone designing a questionnaire?

b) In your field of study, what kind of questionnaires (if any) might be part of research?

Useful language

Task 2

With a partner, practise the expressions below with reference to the information in the table you saw in Unit 7.

Table 7.1: Women at work in the UK in 1975 and 2006

	1975	2006
Women in employment	9.1 million	12.5 million
Full-time gender pay gap	29%	17.1%
Part-time gender pay gap	42%	38.4%
Working mothers	47%	66%
Working mothers with pre-school children	25%	52%
Mothers back at work eight months after giving birth	15%	70%
Female managers	1.8%	33.1%
Female directors	0.6%	14.4%

Source: Equal Opportunities Commission - *Guardian* 14/01/06

Look at the expressions of quantity below (See the *Useful language* box in Unit 8 Task 1.5).

approximately approaching just under just over
a quarter three-quarters a third two-thirds a half

Fill in the gaps below, using expressions of quantity.

a) _____ of managers were female in 2006.

b) _____ of the workforce were working mothers with pre-school children in 1975.

Try to make more sentences to describe the information in the table, using the quantity expressions in the box.

Vocabulary

Task 3

Check that you remember the meaning of the words in the box below, according to how they are used in Units 7 and 8.

> **a curriculum vitae (n)**   **to consult (v) a source**   **to pilot (v) a questionnaire**
> **to administer (v) a questionnaire**   **the implications (n) of the data**
> **to evaluate (v) a solution**

Task 4

Work with a partner. Look at the vocabulary below. Check that you remember the meaning of the words.

Unit 7: The world of work
teleworking
to work flexi-time
the 24/7 economy
ethical working practices

Unit 8: The environment
fossil fuels
deforestation
cyber-crime
endangered languages

Student A: Choose any three of the words or expressions and define them to Student B.

Student B: Close your book. Listen to the definitions given by Student A. What word or phrase is he/she defining?

Change roles. Student B chooses three more words to define.

9 Science and the paranormal

In this unit you will:
- practise language for expressing differing degrees of belief;
- practise presenting a research proposal to a group of colleagues;
- consider the criteria for a good research proposal.

Thinking rationally

At university you are encouraged to think critically and take an analytical approach to issues. There is an emphasis on being able to explain things rationally. However, there are some issues that cannot be explained rationally, e.g., psychic phenomena. For many people, lack of a rational explanation does not make this phenomena any less real.

Task 1: The view of scientists

1.1 Below is a list of quotations which appeared in *The Guardian* newspaper in April 2005. Well-known scientists were asked: "What is the one thing everyone should learn about science?" Which comes closest to your belief about what science should teach?

A

" Science is about uncertainty. We do not yet know the answers to most of the most important questions. "

Freeman Dyson, Emeritus professor of physics at the Institute for Advanced Study, Princeton.

B

" I would teach the world that science is the best way to understand the world, and that for any set of observations, there is only one correct explanation. "

Lewis Wolpert, Emeritus professor of biology as applied to medicine at University College London.

C

" I would teach the world that scientists start by trying very hard to disprove what they hope is true ... A scientist always acknowledges the possibility of error, and is less likely to be mistaken than one who always claims to be right. "

Anthony Hoare, senior researcher at Microsoft Corporation.

D

> " I would teach the world that science = imagination + humility. "
>
> **Michael Baum, Emeritus professor of surgery and visiting professor of medical humanities at University College London.**

E

> " Paranormal phenomena do not exist. Magic, witchcraft, mind-reading, clairvoyance, faith healing and similar practices do not work and never have worked. "
>
> **Roderich Tumulka, researcher in physics at the Mathematics Institute at the University of Tubingen.**

1.2 Which of the above statements appear to contradict one another? Which statements support one another?

1.3 Read the following quotation. Do you share this view?

> Truth is important, we value it. The whole basis for civilisation is the quest for knowledge. Critical thinking and rational science are important in helping us determine what is true and false.
>
> **BBC Radio 4 Leading Edge (11/07/2002).**

1.4 Read the following statements. Discuss your views in pairs. Try to give examples in support of your views.

> If a phenomenon cannot be proved scientifically, then we should not believe it.

> Some phenomena exist which science cannot explain.

Task 2: Local beliefs

Traditional beliefs relating to areas such as healing and medicine are still common.

a) What kinds of traditional beliefs are common in your country?

b) Are there some areas where people believe more in traditional medicine, or believe in phenomena such as witchcraft and magic?

Task 3: Personal beliefs in phenomena

3.1 Do you believe in any of these phenomena?

> telepathy   ghosts/haunted houses
> mind control   hypnosis   astrology
> fortune-telling   alien abductions
> UFOs   healing/alternative medicine
> acupuncture   reincarnation

Useful language: Expressing doubt and belief

I don't believe in this/in these!

They don't exist.

It can't possibly be true …

It might be true …

There might be something in it …

I believe it does/might work.

3.2 What alternative explanations might there be for any of the phenomena in Task 3.1?

For example:

Alien abductions: Many people claim to have been kidnapped by aliens. Here are some possible interpretations of these claims:

- the claims are true;

- people are lying, e.g., to gain attention;

- they are imagining it – it's a delusion;

- there is a scientific explanation, e.g., Chris French, head of psychology research at Goldsmith's College London, states that the experience is due to a condition known as 'sleep paralysis'. When this happens, people are temporarily trapped between being asleep and being awake, and cannot move. They often see and hear things which they are convinced are real. (*Guardian* 26/10/2005)

3.3 Do you know of any research that has been done to prove whether any of the phenomena in Task 3.1 are true or false?

To test the existence of telepathy, for example, researchers at the University of Edinburgh put two subjects in separate sealed rooms. One subject was shown photographs and videos and tried to "communicate" these to the other subject. The other subject had to draw pictures of whatever came into their mind. Researchers looked to see if there was any statistically significant correspondence between the "sent" and "received" images.

In small groups, choose one of the other phenomena in Task 3.1 and discuss how you could "test" whether it exists or not. What type of experiment could you design?

3.4 Listen and comment on the experiments proposed by the other groups.

> **Presentation Skills:** At higher levels of academic study, you may have to carry out some original research. You may have to present your research proposal to your tutors and peers. Tasks 4 and 5 look at these types of presentations. However, the type of presentation may vary according to the department you are in, so it is important to check the criteria expected by your particular department.

Task 4: Research project

On your future academic courses, especially for students of Masters or PhD, presenting a research proposal is common. This involves presenting what you plan to write about/research. Your colleagues and tutors respond by commenting and giving feedback to help develop the proposal.

The following factors need to be considered when conducting an experiment.

- experimental groups and control groups;
- number of subjects;
- statistical significance;
- variables;
- recommendations for further research.

Are such experiments carried out by people conducting research in your area of study? If so, what kinds of theory are they hoping to prove/disprove?

Some departments, however, do not lend themselves to experiment, but rather a paper which relates theory to practice. Below is a list of headings which a student might be expected to use. (This will vary according to the department where you study.)

Title

Rationale for the study (Background information and the overall aim of the research.)

Proposed research questions (Specific questions which the research hopes to answer.)

Methods of data collection (This could include questionnaires, interviews or simply collecting information from different sources.)

For a sample proposal, see Appendix 6.

Task 5: Presentation of a research proposal

Prepare a short research proposal, either for an experiment or for a paper, according to your area of study.

a) Use the headings listed in Task 4 (or if you have the criteria from your future department you can use these headings) and make notes under each heading.

b) Present your proposal to your group.

c) Listen to the proposals given by the rest of the group and evaluate the design of the proposal, e.g., are there any obvious weaknesses in the proposal? Use the Audience feedback sheet in Appendix 8g to give your feedback. Your teacher will give you copies.

10 Studying in a new environment

In this unit you will:
● practise exchanging information;
● reflect on what you have gained from your time on this course;
● reflect on the skills you have developed on the course and how you can continue to develop them.

The importance of reflection

An important part of learning is to reflect on your experience, what you have learnt and how you have learnt it. You should try to do this regularly with recent learning experiences, as you did with the learner diaries, as well as taking a longer perspective (e.g., what you have learnt over a whole course). This unit asks you to look at the long-term perspective.

Task 1: Looking back

Many of you will have been settling into a new environment while using this book – a new college or university, perhaps in a new city or country. Think back over your first few weeks or months in the new environment and note down:

a) two aspects of life that you have found surprising during your time here;

b) two aspects of life that you have enjoyed;

c) two aspects of life that you have found difficult.

Prepare to explain them to other members of the class.

Task 2: Stages in culture shock

2.1 A number of psychological studies claim that people's reactions tend to follow a common pattern while they are settling into a new environment. Read the descriptions in the table below of the five stages identified by Jane Woolfenden. Decide on their chronological order and write the numbers 1 to 5 in the left-hand column of the table.

Stage no.	Description of stage
	You thought you had got used to it, but one or two minor things go wrong and it feels as if the whole world is against you. Some people give up at this stage, or become aggressive or withdrawn.
	Excitement.
	Adjustment to the new environment takes place. You either integrate into the new culture, or decide that you don't like it but have to tolerate it temporarily.
	You begin to get used to it.
	Culture shock. A few things start to go wrong. Differences between your own culture and the new culture start to cause problems. What was once new and exciting now seems unfamiliar and frustrating.

Source: Woolfenden, J. (1990). *How to study and live in Britain.* Northcote House.

2.2 Discuss your choices with a partner. In what way is your experience:

    a) similar to the model?

    b) different from the model?

2.3 Identify the most difficult stage in the process. What advice would your group give to someone going through this stage?

Task 3: Listening

3.1 Listen to either Text 1 (Li) or Text 2 (Chris). The speaker in each case is someone who recently completed a postgraduate degree at a British university. They talk about the challenges that face international students and they offer some advice to those who are about to start a course. Take notes on the advice given by the speaker in your text, so that afterwards you will be able to explain it to someone who has not listened to it.

3.2 Compare notes with someone who listened to the same text. Try to clarify between you any uncertainties that arise.

3.3 Pair up with someone who listened to the other text in Task 3.1. Take it in turns to find out what advice was given in the other text and note the advice down. When your partner is telling you about the other text, wait for an appropriate break between points or sections and then summarise, to check that you have understood the point(s).

3.4 Discuss the relative value of the various pieces of advice and rank them by numbering them 1, 2, 3, etc (1 = most important).

Task 4: Advice for international students

4.1 Draft an advice sheet for newly arrived international students who have got only three or four days to settle in before they start a 12-month course at the school or university where you are studying. Make use of the notes you made in the previous task and of your own experience as an international student.

4.2 Transfer the main headings from your advice sheet to a poster, PowerPoint slide or OHT.

4.3 One member of each group presents the group's advice sheet to the whole class, using the visual aid prepared in Task 4.2.

4.4 With the other members of the class, decide which group's advice sheet would actually be of most use to the newly arrived international students.

Task 5: Assessing your progress

5.1 Estimate your *current* level in each micro-skill listed in the table below. (Tick a box on each line, where 1 = poor; 5 = very good.)

		1	2	3	4	5
1	I can use language appropriate to participation in a discussion, e.g., clarifying what someone has said, giving a counter-opinion.					
2	I can present an article to the class.					
3	I can lead a seminar (group discussion).					
4	I can easily participate in a seminar discussion.					
5	I can put forward a point and develop my ideas.					
6	I can use a text to support my ideas.					
7	I can discuss an article and give my opinion in a seminar on pre-assigned articles I have read.					
8	I can build on what previous speakers have said in a discussion and add to it.					
9	I can plan an effective presentation.					
10	I can give a formal presentation using appropriate signposting.					
11	I can use PowerPoint effectively to support my presentation.					

5.2 Compare your completed tables in pairs or small groups. In what areas do you feel you have made the most progress?

5.3 In your own time, look at Appendix 7 and underline those expressions which you remember using on this course.

Task 6: Ideas for future study

For some students, when you finish this course, your formal learning of English will draw to a close. However, there are still many areas of speaking English you need to develop; what are these areas, and how do you plan to keep working on them?

Area to work on	How to do this

Learner diary

Make an entry in your learner diary, with some concluding reflections on your progress in speaking on this course. You can base your entry on your responses to Tasks 5 and 6 above.

If you find it beneficial, continue using your diary after the course has finished. You can reflect on your further progress in English, particularly if you follow up your plans from Task 6 above.

Key skills

With a partner, discuss the following questions.

a) What criteria are used to evaluate how good a research proposal is in your department? (You may need to consult the Departmental Handbook for this.)

b) During this course, how have you best developed in your ability to:

  • participate in a discussion or seminar?

  • prepare and give a presentation?

Useful language

Work in pairs. Look at the list of phenomena and the *Useful language* box in Unit 9 Task 3.

Student A: Give your opinion on two of the phenomena listed. Do you believe in it/them or not?

Student B: Respond using one of the expressions from the box.

Change roles.

Remember that expressions of disbelief are very strong, so make sure your voice conveys this!

Vocabulary

In pairs, discuss how each of the words in the box below is related to conducting research.

statistical significance	data collection	variables	rationale	research proposal

NET EFFECTS

OVER the past 30 years, the writing and design of postgraduate courses and learning materials has changed enormously as universities have realised distance learners need much more than a tutor who marks assignments and 5 sends them back. Many organisations now provide summer schools and social events for students, creating a virtual learning community. But it's e-mail and the Internet which now offer the most exciting possibilities.

VIA the Internet, distance learners can formulate their own 10 curriculum, learn at their own pace and set their own timetable. And regular e-mail correspondence with a tutor can be much more productive and rewarding than infrequent tutorials.

THE variety of media that online courses can offer means 15 that distance learning can be a rich, inspiring experience. Graphics, sound and video bring dry texts to life and students can choose to spend more time going into depth on particular subjects which they find difficult to grasp by hyperlinking to other pages on the CD-ROM or website. 20 Unlike the slower paper-based courses, e-mail access means tutors and fellow students can help quickly with queries.

THE Open University was a pioneer of distance learning and remains the biggest online provider with more than 25 degrees wholly online as well as many others with online content.

25 **SOME** online postgraduate courses offer students access to information that might prove difficult to research if all they had available was the university library. The University of Surrey's online MBA, for example, has links to the university's learning resources department, a full range of academic 30 journals and even Reuters business information.

Source: Staff. (2004, January 24). Net Effects. *The Guardian*.

E FOR DEGREE

Online studying is allowing graduates to continue in education while working

By Stephen Hoare

Graduates wanting to study for a
5 further qualification no longer have to
delay their entry into the job market
and the opportunity to start repaying
their student loans.

Many are opting to study for a masters
10 degree or postgraduate qualification
online, enabling them to combine study
with a full-time career.

The Guardian's education website reveals
a number of universities offering online
15 postgraduate courses in business,
electronic commerce, Internet systems
development, online education and even
sociology – areas that make heavy use of
Internet technology. Most are at masters
20 or diploma level.

The biggest online provider is the Open
University, which has 22,000
postgraduates worldwide and offers
more than 25 degrees wholly online as
25 well as many others with online content.
OU pro-vice-chancellor, Professor Linda
Jones, says: "Online links generally with
the advantages of Open University study.
Students can be very flexible and fit

30 study around personal circumstances.
Over 70 per cent of our students work
full-time and many are sponsored by their
employers, who enjoy the benefits of
developing the skills of their workforce."

35 The OU has discovered that take-up of
online postgraduate degrees is enhanced
by technical support such as online
conferencing and student discussion
groups, as well as an efficient online
40 registration and tracking system. All online
students are offered personal tutorials.

Online and distance learning provider
Pearson Education runs the highly
successful Herriot-Watt business school
45 MBA, and has teamed up with Portsmouth
University to offer an online MSc in
electronic commerce and marketing and
Internet systems development. Now
entering their second year, the Portsmouth
50 online postgrad courses have attracted

mainly UK students, but with growing numbers from Africa and Asia.

A spokesperson for Pearson's distributed learning division says: "We have identified
55 e-courses as a growth area and the degrees we have developed with Portsmouth appeal mainly to people who are working. Most are on a career path and have been out of full-time education
60 for several years."

With the university taking care of course content and the accreditation, and Pearson adding marketing expertise, an Internet platform and technical support,
65 Portsmouth's online students benefit from tried and tested distance learning techniques. Online also has the added advantage of enabling academics to update course material. A spokesperson
70 says: "Being online allows us to update once or twice a term."

Advantages vary, but a major attraction is flexibility. Students can complete an online degree over a longer timespan –
75 possibly taking a mix and match of modules. Online is also suited to short

but intensive certificate courses such as the certificate in online learning offered by London University's Institute of
80 Education.

Senior lecturer Anita Pincas says: "Online study makes it so much easier to deal with the huge numbers of students on today's campus. There's no way the
85 teacher can see everyone. Plus it's very difficult for students to collaborate with each other if they are busy with lectures and seminars. Virtual meetings add to what students can do."

90 Some online postgraduate courses offer students access to information that might prove difficult to research if all they had available was the university library. The University of Surrey management
95 school's online MBA, now about to enter its third year, has links to the university's learning resources department, a full range of academic journals and even Reuters business information.
100 Commercial director Chris Croker says: "We give our students a laptop pre-loaded with all the multimedia course material, access to over 1,400 management journals and even access
105 to our students' union. The only thing they can't do is buy a round of drinks!"

E FOR DEGREE

Source: Hoare, S. (2003, August 26). E for Degree. *The Guardian*.

Men want to be househusbands

Not so long ago, the idea of fathers staying at home to be full-time childcarers was not common, but new statistics show this situation
5 is rapidly changing.

According to latest Government statistics, in 2001 there were around 155,000 men staying at home full-time to look after children or home, with
10 60 per cent doing so completely voluntarily. Added to this is the growing number of men who are working part-time or flexi-hours in order to take on the job of chief carer.
15 A poll of 2,000 pregnant women and their partners, published by *Pregnancy and Birth*, reveals that most men want to spend more time with their children. In the poll, only 34 per cent
20 of men wanted to continue in full-time work once they had children, with 33 per cent preferring to go part-time and another third prepared to become stay-at-home fathers. The only thing
25 keeping them from staying at home is money – the biggest concern for most prospective fathers, who said financial fears caused them more anxiety than worries about the loss of their freedom.

30 The social stigma around giving up work to raise a family – which applies almost exclusively to men – is fading away. There are many more fathers to be seen at playgroups and schools,
35 dropping off and picking up, in between running the family home. There is a growing need for more resources for stay-at-home fathers, such as the website launched by two
40 full-time fathers: www.homedad.org. uk. According to one of the founders of the site, "almost all resources for parents are aimed primarily at mothers. Although we were constantly
45 being told in the media that the number of stay-at-home dads was rising, we felt we didn't have a voice." He claims that the website, which has over 500 members, is currently the
50 only UK support group dedicated to helping dads who are staying at home to bring up their children.

Based on:
Pereira H. Stay-at-home dads. Retrieved May 10, 2005, from http://www.ivillage.co.uk/parenting/pracad/parcare/ articles/0,,186674_618693-1,00.html [URL no longer active]
and
Author unknown. (2004, August 15). Men want to be househusbands. Retrieved May 15, 2005, from http://www.uominicasalinghi.it/ index.asp?pg=1030

Family formation

With the exception of the periods immediately
after the two world wars, few births occurred
outside marriage during the first 60 years of the
20th century. During the 1960s and 1970s such
5 births became more common. In 2003 most children
were born to married couples, but around 41 per
cent of births in the United Kingdom occurred
outside marriage.

Most of the increase in the number of births
10 outside marriage has been due to an increase in
the proportion of children born to cohabiting
couples. In most European countries there have
been significant increases since 1980 in the
proportions of births occurring outside marriage.
15 However, there are large differences between
countries. In 2003, over half of births in Sweden
and Estonia occurred outside marriage (56 per cent
in both countries) compared with only 4 per cent
of births in both Greece and Cyprus.

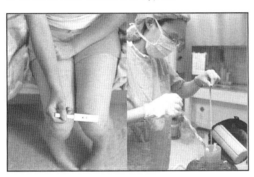

20 The rate of multiple births in the United Kingdom
increased from 12.8 per 1,000 of all maternities
in 1993 to 14.8 per 1,000 of all maternities in
2003. The greater use of fertility treatment is an
important factor. In 2003, twins were born at a rate
25 of 14.7 per 1,000 maternities, while 0.2 per 1,000
maternities led to triplets or more. Multi-birth rates
are highest for women over the age of 35. Among
women aged 35 to 39 years, twins accounted for
21.2 per 1,000 maternities, and triplets for 0.3 per
30 1,000 maternities. In comparison, for women aged
under 20, the rates were 6.5 and 0.1 respectively.

There has been an increase in the age of women
at childbirth. In England and Wales the average age
of married women giving birth for the first time
35 has increased by nearly six years since 1971, to 29.9
in 2003. The average age of fathers at childbirth
also rose, from 29.2 years in 1971 to 32.7 years in
2003. Births outside marriage tend to take place
at a younger age than those inside marriage. In
40 2003 women giving birth outside marriage were
around four years younger than those giving birth
inside marriage.

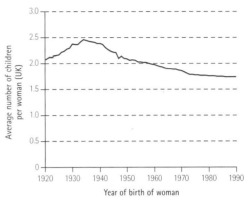

Source: Office for National Statistics; Government Actuary's Dept.

In the United Kingdom the average number of
children per woman (family size) increased from
45 2.07 children for women born in 1920 to a peak
of 2.46 children for women born in 1934. This peak
corresponds with the 1960s 'baby boom'. Family
size declined for subsequent generations and is
projected to decline to around 1.74 children for
50 women born in the mid-1980s. Women born in
1955, and now at the end of their childbearing
years, had an average of 2.03 children. The decline
in family size among women born in the mid-1930s
onwards is the result both of fewer women having
55 large families and more women remaining childless.
In England and Wales, 31 per cent of women born
in 1920 had given birth to three or more children
by the end of their childbearing years. This increased
to around 40 per cent of women born in the 1930s.
60 It then dropped rapidly to a level of around 30 per
cent, where it has remained for the 1945-born
generation onwards. Women in England and Wales
born since the Second World War have waited
longer before starting a family. Thirty eight per cent
65 of women born in 1948 were still childless at age
25; this increased to 65 per cent of women aged
25 born in 1978.

Another way in which people may extend their
families is through adoption. In 2003 there were
70 4,800 adoptions in England and Wales, with 47 per
cent of adopted children aged between one and
four years old. Increased use of contraception,
new abortion laws and changed attitudes towards
lone motherhood have meant that 16,700 fewer
75 children were adopted in 2003 than in 1971.
Most of the children adopted since 1971 were
born outside marriage.

Adapted from:
Cook, L. & Martin, J. (2005, March 22). Chapter 2: Households and
Families. In Social Trends 35: 2005 edition. Retrieved May 20, 2005,
from http://www.statistics.gov.uk/downloads/theme_social/
Social_Trends35/Social_Trends_35_Ch02.pdf [URL no longer active].

PARTNERSHIPS

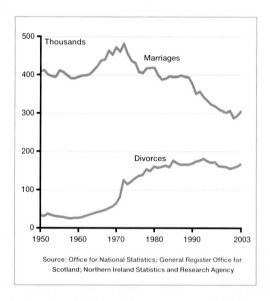

The pattern of partnership formation has changed since the early 1970s but, despite the decrease in the overall numbers of people marrying, marriage is still the most common form of partnership for men and women. In 2003 around half of the UK population were married.

In 1950 there were 408,000 marriages in the United Kingdom. The number grew during the mid- to late-1960s to reach a peak of 480,000 in 1972. This growth was partly a result of the babies born in the post-war boom reaching marriageable ages and, at that time, people were marrying younger than in more recent years. The annual number of marriages then began to decline and in 2003 there were just over 306,000. This was the second successive annual rise.

The number of divorces taking place each year in Great Britain more than doubled between 1958 and 1969. By 1972 the number of divorces in the United Kingdom had doubled again. Although there was a slight drop in the number of divorces in 1973, the number rose again in 1974 and peaked in 1993 at 180,000. The number of divorces then fell to 155,000 in 2000. In 2003 the number of divorces increased by 4 per cent to 167,000, from 161,000 in 2002. This was the third successive annual rise.

Following divorce, people often form new relationships and may remarry. Remarriages, for one or both partners, increased by a third between 1971 and 1972 after the introduction of the Divorce Reform Act 1969, and peaked at 141,000 in 1988. In 2003 there were just over 123,000 remarriages, accounting for two fifths of all marriages.

Source: Office for National Statistics; General Register Office for Scotland; Northern Ireland Statistics and Research Agency

The age at which people get married for the first time has continued to increase. In 1971 the average age at first marriage was 25 for men and 23 for women in England and Wales and this increased to 31 for men and 29 for women in 2003. There has been a similar trend across Europe. Between 1971 and 2002, the average age at first marriage in the European Union increased from 26 to 30 for men and 23 to 27 for women. However there are differences between the EU countries. In 2002 the country with the youngest newly-weds was Lithuania (26 for men and 24 for women) while Sweden had the oldest (33 for men and 30 for women).

Traditionally women have married men who are older than themselves. The average age difference between partners in first marriages ranged from just under two years between partners in Ireland and in Portugal to just under four years in Greece. In England and Wales, the majority of women marry men older than themselves. However, an increasing proportion of women are marrying younger men. The proportion of couples where the husband was younger than the wife increased from 15 per cent for those who married in 1963 to 26 per cent for those who married in 2001. Over the same period, the proportion of couples where the man was at most five years older than the woman fell from just under two thirds in 1963 to just under a half in 2001. The proportion of marriages where the man was more than five years older than the woman increased from 21 per cent in 1963 to 26 per cent in 2001.

changes in the family environment since the early 1970s. The number of children aged under 16 in England and Wales who experienced the divorce of their parents peaked at almost 176,000 in 1993. This fell to 142,000 in 2000, and then increased each year up to 2003. Just over one-fifth of children affected by divorce in 2003 were under five years old and nearly two-thirds were aged ten or under. Children are living in an increasing variety of different family

Age gap between males and females at marriage		
England & Wales	Percentage	
	1963	2001
Man younger	15	26
Man 0-5 years older	64	48
Man at least 6 years older	21	26

Source: Office for National Statistics

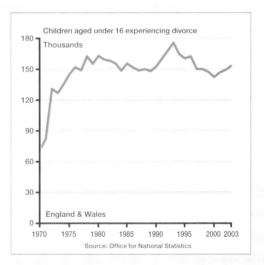

Children aged under 16 experiencing divorce
Thousands
England & Wales
Source: Office for National Statistics

structures during their lives. Parents separating can result in lone-parent families, and new relationships can create stepfamilies. Children tend to stay with their mother following the break-up of a partnership. In 2003/04 the vast majority (83 per cent) of stepfamilies in Great Britain consisted of a stepfather and natural mother.

The trend towards marrying later in life may, in part, be explained by the rise in cohabitation. The percentage of non-married men and women under the age of 60 cohabiting in Great Britain more than doubled between 1986 (the earliest year data are available on a consistent basis) and 2003/04, to 25 per cent and 27 per cent respectively.

Changes in patterns of cohabitation, marriage and divorce have led to considerable

Adapted from:
Cook, L. & Martin, J. (2005, March 22). Chapter 2: Households and Families. In Social Trends 35: 2005 edition. Retrieved May 20, 2005, from http://www.statistics.gov.uk/downloads/theme_social/ Social_Trends35/Social_Trends_35_Ch02.pdf [URL no longer active].

Household composition

There were 24.1 million households in Great Britain in spring 2004. Although the population has been increasing, the number of 5 households has increased faster due to the trend towards smaller household sizes. The population grew by 6 per cent between 1971 and 2003, while the number of households increased 10 by 32 per cent. The average household size fell over this period from 2.9 to 2.4 people. More lone-parent families, smaller family sizes, and the increase in one-person households has driven this decrease.

There has been a decrease in the proportion of households containing the traditional family unit – couple families with dependent 15 children – and an increase in the proportion of lone-parent families. The proportion of households in Great Britain comprising a couple with dependent children fell from over one-third in 1971 to just over one-fifth in 2004. Over the same period, the proportion comprising a lone-parent household with dependent children doubled, to seven 20 per cent of households in 2004. Since 1971 the proportion of people living in the 'traditional' family household of a couple with dependent children has fallen from just over one-half to under two-fifths, while the proportion of people living in couple family households with no children has increased from almost one-fifth to one-quarter. One in 25 eight people lived in a lone-parent household in spring 2004 – three times the proportion in 1971.

Since the early 1970s, there has been a fall in the percentage of dependent children living in families headed by a couple, and an increase in those living in lone-parent families. In spring 2004, 76 per cent of children lived in a family unit headed by a couple. The 30 proportion of children living in lone-parent families tripled between 1972 and spring 2004, to 24 per cent. Lone mothers head around nine out of ten lone-parent families.

One of the most notable changes in household composition over the last three decades has been the increase in one-person households. The proportion of such households in Great Britain increased from 18 per cent in 1971 to 29 per cent in 2004. In the 35 mid-1980s and 1990s these households mainly comprised older women. This was a reflection of there being fewer men than women in older age groups and, in particular, the tendency for wives to outlive their husbands. In 2003/04, 60 per cent of women aged 75 and over were living alone, much the same proportion as in 1986/87. There has been an increasing tendency for people to live on their own at younger ages. The largest 40 increases were among people aged 25 to 44 years – the proportions of men and women who lived alone both doubled between 1986/87 and 2003/04.

Another change in family structure and relationships has been the increase in the proportion of adults who live with their parents. Some young people may be delaying leaving home because of 45 economic necessity, such as difficulties entering the housing market. Others may simply choose to continue living with their parents. The later age at marriage may also be a factor. Young men were more likely than young women to live with their parents. In 2004, 58 per of men aged 20 to 24 did so compared with 39 per cent of women 50 of the same age. Between 1991 and 2004 the proportion of men and women in this age group who were living with their parents increased by seven to eight percentage points.

Adapted from:

Cook, L. & Martin, J. (2005, March 22). Chapter 2: Households and Families. In Social Trends 35: 2005 edition.
Retrieved May 20, 2005, from http://www.statistics.gov.uk/downloads/theme_social/ Social_Trends35/Social_Trends_35_Ch02.pdf
[URL no longer active].

SINGLETONS ARE ON THE INCREASE

THE NUMBER OF PEOPLE LIVING ALONE HAS RISEN BY A THIRD SINCE THE SEVENTIES

A recent survey shows that the longer people live by themselves, the more likely they are to keep doing so. However, after the age of 45, there is a gender switch – more women start to leave their partners and live alone, 5 sometimes because children have grown up and left home and their marriages dissolve.

Over the past 30 years, the number of UK households with just one occupant has risen 31 per cent, although the population has grown by only 5 per cent in that period, 10 according to the research, funded by the Economic and Social Research Council, which tracked the lives of more than 150,000 individuals since 1971.

The figures have serious implications for the housing market, with a huge shortage of affordable housing for the 15 young right across the country. However, it also marks the growth of the culture of 'individualisation', with both men and women unwilling to sacrifice their personal freedom - and income – to co-habit or get married.

Research carried out by Malcolm Williams, from the 20 University of Plymouth, reveals that in their late teens and early twenties, both men and women are likely to live by themselves but after 25 men are far more likely to live alone. Williams said: 'All the signs are that the trend towards living alone will continue. Even more socially important is that, 25 once people have gone solo, they are more likely to continue to do so.'

The figures show that in 1971 just 1.6 per cent of people aged between 15 and 44 lived alone, but that this rose to 3.5 per cent in 1981 and to 8.4 per cent by 1991. It is 30 predicted that the next set of figures will show that in 2002 the proportion will have risen again to encompass one-third of all households.

But some experts have argued that it is not necessarily beneficial for people to spend long periods of life by 35 themselves. Solo living is simply the result of greater choice in life, particularly for women, and also the greater fragility in relationships.

Men may be twice as likely as women to be living on their own between the ages of 35 and 44 but are less well suited 40 to the single life. Research published last year showed they had fewer friends and were more likely to have poor diets, suffer from depression and live in less comfortable homes.

Researchers at Edinburgh University said solo living was a growing social trend affecting city populations in particular, but 45 that it had its downside. 'Single professionals often choose to settle and take advantage of a metropolitan lifestyle. What we regard as "the norm" is changing and this has implications for families and relationships as well as working and housing arrangements,' said researcher Adam Smith.

50 Family breakdown has also contributed to the single trend because women are far more likely to keep the children and become lone parents while men move into a flat on their own. Professor Richard Scase, an economist from the University of Kent and author of the report Britain 2010, 55 said: 'Women have the emotional capital to develop and keep friendships and support networks, whereas men tend to become more isolated when living alone without women to arrange their social lives.'

Adapted from: Revill, J. (2005, January 30). Singletons are on the increase. *The Observer.*

Modern-day fathers feel like failures

Today's fathers feel like failures after losing their traditional role as head of the family.

Fatherhood is in crisis, with men admitting they are worse parents than their fathers, that they avoid emotional involvement with their children and use the office to avoid the stress of their home life.

A survey of more than 2,100 British adults found that despite wanting to be good dads, the modern-day father is retreating into the authoritarian model of his fathers' generation.

'Fatherhood is becoming a mild form of depression for the modern-day man, there is a grey cloud that hangs over it,'

'Fatherhood is becoming a mild form of depression for the modern-day man, there is a grey cloud that hangs over it,' said Marian Salzman, chief strategy officer at the advertising and public relations company Euro RSCG Worldwide. 'Society offers no realistic role models for real men trying to do their best,' said Salzman. 'The disappointment and feeling of failure is resulting in men shutting down emotionally because they no longer have the old central role in their family and don't know what other role is available for them.'

Fathers questioned for the survey admitted to being depressed and pessimistic about their parenting skills, with one in five feeling strongly that they were worse parents than their dads had been. They also reported feeling overwhelmed by the multiple duties of work and home: three out of four said they were not in control of their lives and one-third felt desperate to reduce stress.

The keenest desire of fathers is to simplify their lives after having children and, to do that, they end up attempting to escape the demands of their families by hiding in the workplace. Almost one in

four wanted less holiday time than before they became fathers. 'This may be because their desire for holiday is tempered by thoughts of the
40 cost and effort of taking the family on holiday, or because staying home is anything but relaxing,' said Salzman. 'But the result is that dads are slipping into a more distant, conservative role that is more about discipline and the sterner
45 expression of love, such as that expressed through helping with schoolwork.'

Jack O'Sullivan, director of the national lobby group Fathers Direct, believes that society's definition of fatherhood and fathering is filled
50 with contradictions. 'Society is alienating fathers from their children,' he said. 'While there are clear demands for fathers to be more involved in family life, there is an absence of roles for them to take. 'The survey found that, feeling that they
55 have failed to be the fathers they hoped, modern dads are increasingly avoiding emotional involvement with their children: one-quarter said they never talked about personal issues with their child at all. Instead, the survey found, dads
60 try to bond with their children through schoolwork, with more than half claiming they were more involved in their children's learning than their parents had been. 'The adoption of a less emotional expression of love seems to make
65 men more likely to support physical punishment of children,' said Salzman. 'Half of dads agreed with spanking, compared to just over one-third of mothers, a belief which is likely to alienate fathers from their children even more.'

70 Professor Laurie Taylor believes that the status of fatherhood has been undermined by modern life. 'Fathers have not quite been abolished but they are further away from their children than ever before,' he said. 'In the past, sons duplicated
75 their own father and looked to him to emulate his job and his wisdom. 'Now, however, fathers have nothing for their children to inherit – the world is changing too quickly and, instead of sitting at their fathers' feet listening to their stories about
80 the world, children are closed up in their own rooms on the Internet, finding out about it first. It is difficult to know how to reassert the role of fatherhood. There is nothing obvious for him to do or be.'

'Society is alienating fathers from their children'

Adapted from: Hill, R. (2004, June 20). How New Man turned into distant, confused New Dad. *The Guardian.*

Affluent but Anxious and Alienated

A far-reaching survey over decades finds Britons better off but more unhappy.

Despite higher incomes, better health and much greater opportunity for women, Britons are increasingly depressed,
5 unhappy in their relationships, and alienated from civic society, according to an exhaustive study to be published next week.

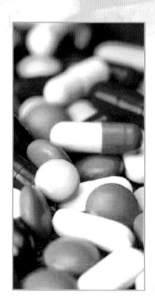

The latest findings come from three pioneering studies, which have been following the lives of everyone born in England, Scotland and Wales in one week in 1946, 1958 and 1950 –
10 more than 40,000 people.

The study, Changing Britain, Changing Lives, is the first to compare in detail the results of the three studies. It identifies a society more fractured and individualistic, but where people at the same time find their success, wealth and opportunity
15 dependent on family background to an even greater extent.

Fourteen per cent of men born in 1970 were as likely to admit to depression and anxiety in 2000, compared with only seven per cent of the 1958 group in 1991. For women the differences in the same years were almost as dramatic – 20 per cent in
20 2000 and 12 per cent in 1991.

Of those born in 1970, 22 per cent of men and 24 per cent of women admitted to being unhappy with their first marriage in their early 30s, compared with just three per cent of men and two per cent of women of those born in 1958 at the same age.
25 Single people too were similarly much more likely to be unhappy with their lives.

Those born later stay in the family home for longer periods because of the rising cost of housing. They also increasingly delay parenthood until their late 30s and early 40s, at a point
30 when their own parents become in need of support. They then have to look after their own children and support their parents at the same time, and are unlikely to enjoy the extended period of freedom from dependency enjoyed by adults in the past.

Ninety per cent of women and 80 per cent of men among the
35 1946 group had become parents by the age 30. However, this
was true of only 30 per cent of men and 52 per cent of women
among those born in 1970.

The "striking increase" in women entering higher education
and establishing themselves in the labour market has led to
40 relationships and parenthood coming later. Three-quarters of
30-year-old women were in employment in 2000, compared
with half of those aged 32 in 1978.

Average female earnings were almost twice as high for 30-year-
olds born in 1970 than for those born in 1946, although most
45 top jobs still went to men. The growing financial independence
of women also "means that economic considerations were less
likely to force them to remain in unhappy partnerships".

Women transformed their position, obtaining more higher
qualifications and staying on in education longer than men by
50 1970. Across both sexes, the percentages gaining a degree
quadrupled between the 1946 and 1970 groups, while the
proportions leaving with no qualifications plummeted from
40 per cent to 10 per cent.

But in education and employment, class remained a dominant
55 factor. "Those at the bottom end of the socioeconomic scale
manifested little evidence of the rising standards enjoyed by
the majority," the study says.

Rising house prices put owner-occupation out of reach, and
relative poverty was increasing. The study concludes: "Our
60 findings give few grounds for optimism that these disparities
are disappearing, or even diminishing. Despite rising education
levels and rising affluence ... the old polarities based on social
class appear, if anything to be strengthening."

Source: Woodward, W. (2003, February 22). Affluent but anxious
and alienated. *The Guardian.*

The latest research on babies and how their brains develop shows that the attention that we receive as babies impacts
5 on our brain structures. If we find ourselves cared for by people who love us, and who are highly sensitive to our unique personalities, the
10 pleasure of those relationships will help to trigger the development of the "social brain". In the simplest terms, the prefrontal cortex (and in
15 particular its orbitofrontal area) plays a major role in managing our emotional lives: it picks up on social cues, the non-verbal messages
20 that other people transmit; it enables us to empathise, as well as playing an important part in restraining our primitive emotional impulse.

25 Surprising as it may seem, we are not born with these capacities: this part of the brain develops almost entirely post-natally Nor is it just a
30 matter of waiting for your baby to develop an orbitofrontal cortex so it can

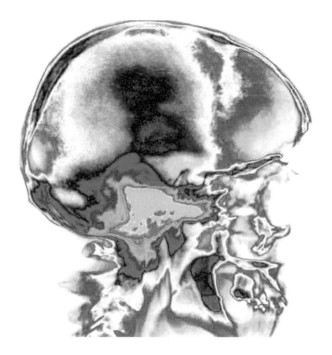

Cradle of civilisation

begin to relate well to others. There is nothing automatic about it. Instead, the kind of brain that each baby develops is the brain
35 that comes out of his or her experiences with other people. Love facilitates a massive burst of connections in this part of the brain between six and 12 months. Neglect at this time can greatly reduce the development of the pre-frontal cortex.

Early care also establishes the way we deal with stress. Babies
40 rely on their carers to soothe distress and restore equilibrium. With responsive parents, the stress response, a complex chain of biochemical reactions, remains an emergency response. However, being with caregivers who convey hostility or resentment at a baby's needs, or who ignore their baby or leave him in a state
45 of distress for longer than he can bear, will make a baby's stress response over-sensitive. Recent research by Marilyn Essex at the University of Wisconsin shows that children who lived with a depressed parent in infancy are more reactive to stress later in life; children who lived with a depressed parent later in
50 childhood showed no such effect.

This makes sense in evolutionary terms to have newborn brains which are unfinished, because they can be adapted to fit the needs of the social group. In effect, they can be programmed to behave in ways that suit their community. However, it is a risky
55 strategy. In a harsh environment, a baby's cries may be ignored,

or he may be punished for being distressed. This is likely to produce an individual who becomes, in his turn, relatively insensitive and prone to aggression – and this could be useful in a tense, hostile community. Researchers have found clear links between harsh
60 treatment in the first two years and later antisocial behaviour.

This research has relevance to two current debates – on smacking and nurseries. Looked at from this perspective, one can clearly see that smacking is damaging. Furthermore, nurseries may not provide the things that babies need most: being held and
65 cuddled; having someone familiar and safe to notice how you feel, someone who can quickly put things right when they go wrong, someone who smiles at you lovingly. On the contrary, it is likely that babies in a nursery will find that they are not special to anyone in that way that parents believe their own children are,
70 and they will have to wait for attention. One close observational study of a local authority nursery found that there was little or no eye contact, and little holding or comforting.

The research bears out the effects of such nurseries on babies. Babies can only cope with about ten hours a week of daycare
75 before it may start to affect their emotional development, particularly if the care is of low quality. The strongest research findings are that full-time care during the first and second years is strongly linked to later behaviour problems. These are the children who are "mean" to others, who hit and blame other
80 children. They are likely to be less cooperative and more intolerant of frustration. These are all capacities which suggest poor development of the "social brain". Evidence that increasing the caregiver/baby ratio in nurseries does reduce problems of aggression confirms that these children have simply not had
85 enough loving, individual attention.

These findings are not good news for working parents or for single parents who want to return to work. These parents may end up putting their babies into poor-quality, full-time nursery care before the age of six months. It is their children whose emotional and social development could be affected – not those of better-off parents who can afford to work part-time or buy in the highest
90 quality care. This is not a solution that benefits society in the long-term. The science is there, demonstrating the vulnerability of a baby's neurobiology; and the social research is there, showing that full-time nurseries are bad for babies.

It is time to think clearly about what our new options might be. Most women don't want to return to an age of compulsory full-time motherhood, especially given the stress and loneliness of being
95 at home with only a baby for company.

On the other hand, we can't afford not to provide the kind of loving one-to-one nurturing that babies need, if we want to have a cooperative, socially skilled society. Most mothers and an increasing number of fathers want to be able to spend time with their babies, and often feel that they lose touch with their babies if they work full-time.

100 We have to come up with new flexible solutions, such as extended paid parental leave, that enable both parents to be involved with their baby while keeping the family economy afloat. We need to ensure that our nurseries are of the highest quality. We also need more community involvement to prevent early parenthood from being isolated and miserable. By investing our time and money in the first two years of life, we will be repaid in greater social stability.

Source: Gerhardt, S. (2004, July 24). Cradle of Civilisation. *The Guardian*.

Employers urged to help fight obesity

The government today called on employers and schools to help fight the growing problem of obesity in the UK.

Speaking at a summit in London on diet and exercise, public health minister Melanie Johnson said she was "disappointed" by the lack of progress made by the food industry in reducing salt content.

Last year Ms Johnson demanded evidence of action from the industry
5 after raising concerns about the impact over-consumption of salt was having on people's diets.

The Department of Health has warned that unless companies cut salt levels, it may consider naming and shaming the worst offenders or force products to carry a "high in salt" label.

10 The Food Standards Agency recommends adults and children over the age of 11 consume no more than six grams of salt a day but the current average is nearer ten grams.

Critics have accused the government of producing too many reports on public health but not taking any action to combat problems like obesity.

15 Today Ms Johnson said the possibility of a ban on the advertising of "junk" food during children's television hours was still being considered. And changes to food labelling, such as putting clearer health messages on products, were also being actively considered at a European level, Miss Johnson said.

20 Bosses were urged to provide incentives to staff to adopt a healthy lifestyle, and schools to promote exercise in the playground at break times. The proposals appear in two government public consultation documents on how to encourage people to adopt a more healthy lifestyle.

But Ms Johnson said there was a limit to what the government alone can
25 do to encourage people to keep fit and eat healthily.

She said: "This issue is not just for government – lasting improvements are only achievable if others, including the food industry, consumer groups, health experts and the media work together over the coming years to tackle these issues.

30 "Individuals also have to take responsibility for their diets or those of the people in their charge."

Sports minister Richard Caborn said obesity levels in England had tripled in the last 20 years mainly due to lack of exercise by children and adults. He said: "Creating a more active nation is a priority for the whole of
35 the government."

The chief medical officer for England recommends that adults should do a minimum 30 minutes' exercise five days a week to keep fit while children and young people should aim at completing an hour's moderate exercise every day.

40 Inactivity and obesity are thought to cost Britain more than £10bn a year in the direct costs of treatment and indirect costs through sickness absence.

Adapted from: Andalo, D. (2004, May 26). Employers urged to fight obesity. *The Guardian.*

Stress arises from a number of different factors. For many people stress originates in the work or study situation. For other people it originates in the family, where expectations of family members vary. However, a situation which is stressful for one person will not be stressful for
5 *another. Some people appear by nature to be relaxed in any situation, irrespective of how stressful the situation may appear to others. Stress is essentially what individuals experience when they feel threatened or under pressure. The body responds in particular ways to this experience.*

The causes of stress

Stress

To what extent can it be controlled?

The changing nature of work contributes to stress;
10 in the past, individuals often had the same job for a large proportion of their lives, whereas nowadays it is more common for jobs to be on a more temporary basis. This can be very stressful from a financial point of view, with families to support and mortgage
15 payments to keep up, and individuals constantly concerned about the security of their jobs. The relationship between employer and employee, the pressure of deadlines and competitiveness between employees can all cause stress.

20 For students the impact of stress is most often felt around the exam period; final school exams take on huge importance, as a factor which can determine a person's future. International students who are sponsored by their governments or companies feel a
25 particular stress due to high expectations they need to fulfil, with the extra challenge of dealing with life in a different culture.

For some people, home life may be a source of stress, rather than an escape from it. Family disputes
30 can cause stress, as can the demands of running a home and looking after children.

How to deal with stress

Just as people become stressed in different situations, so their bodies respond in different ways. In order to deal effectively with stress, it is important to identify
35 the symptoms of stress for you as an individual; how does stress manifest itself? It might begin with a feeling of nervousness, an accelerated heart rate and an increase in the rate of breathing. The individual might start to fell tension in the neck or shoulders
40 and a sick feeling in the stomach. Depression, headaches and fatigue may be other responses to stress.

People deal with stress in a variety of ways; some people find meditation a useful way to relax. For other
45 people physical activity is the best stress-reliever, e.g., a work-out in the gym, or an aerobics class can help get rid of the tensions of the day. Being in touch with nature through gardening or walking are other very common ways that people manage stress. Taking
50 deep breaths can be another simple, but effective way of coping.

Finding ways to relax is of course important in managing stress. However, once the triggers of stress have been identified, e.g., a certain situation at work,
55 it is equally important to try and deal with the causes

of the stress, rather than simply relieving the symptoms. In addition, a change in lifestyle may be required to make life less stressful overall.
60 This may involve getting more sleep or changing diet. Ten cups of coffee a day may increase stress levels rather than reduce them.

Generally stress is not something that
65 happens suddenly, but is actually an accumulation of various factors. Awareness of these factors is the first step in determining how to deal with it.

STRESS:
Keep things in perspective

Diagnosing and dealing with stress

According to estimates, around 50 per cent, and in some universities, nearly 70 per cent of students are working part
5 time to support themselves while they study. Add to this, the exams, the debt and the parties and it is easy to see why many students suffer from stress. Although stress is a natural part of life,
10 when it becomes a regular feature it can be debilitating both in terms of health and finances.

The term "stress" is often used quite loosely to describe even a temporary
15 feeling of being under pressure. The technical definition, however, in relation to work or study is "the adverse reaction people have to excessive pressure or other types of demand placed on them".
20 In other words stress is not so much about what you feel when you are under pressure but about how you react.

Diagnosing stress

Successful treatment of any medical
25 condition starts with diagnosis. The same is true of stress. To manage stress successfully you need to be aware of the symptoms. In 'Managing workplace stress' the authors split the symptoms into
30 two categories — physical and behavioural.

Physical symptoms

- Tiredness
- Nausea
35 • Headaches
- Muscle tension
- Nervous twitches
- Altered sleep patterns

Behavioural symptoms

40 • Aggression
- Anxiety
- Poor decision-making
- Inability to prioritise
- Mood changes
45 • Difficulty in concentrating
- Feelings of failure
- Isolation

If you can identify the symptoms of stress or possibly even see an emerging pattern
50 to your stress, you can then start to think about possible causes. For example, does the stress only arise at certain points of the year such as exam season? Do you feel stressed and anxious when you have to
55 deliver presentations?

Techniques for dealing with stress

The first action to take if you recognise that you are suffering from stress is to talk
60 to someone. It could be a family member or friend whom you can trust. Most universities now offer counselling services either as part of the university's own central services or as part of the student's
65 union welfare services. The services on offer may also include access to a peer-mentor or "buddy" who may well be a student on the same course but in a different year. Contact your student union
70 for more details.

One other useful source of support is "Nightline". This unique service operates after 6pm specifically so that students can talk to someone when perhaps access to
75 other support services or even friends is limited. The service is run by students for students and offers a listening ear for a whole range of problems that students may have. Nightline operates nationally
80 and in most universities (www.nightline.ac.uk).

At www.stressbusting.co.uk Dr Roger Henderson, a GP, recommends the following five practical techniques for
85 dealing with stress:

- Keep a diary — use it to log situations, events, times, places and people that appear to cause you stress, then ...

- Talk through your diary with a good
90 friend or partner and ask for impartial advice.

- Learn how to relax — practise deep-breathing techniques such as slowly inhaling while counting to five; hold
95 your breath for five seconds then breath out slowly. Repeat this 10 times when you are feeling stressed and concentrate on nothing but breathing.

- Exercise regularly — brisk walking for
100 20 minutes three times a week.

- Plan breaks in your day — allocate time in the morning and afternoon when you can have time for yourself.

References:
Williams S and Cooper. L. Managing workplace stress. Chichester: John Wiley & Son; 2002.

Adapted from: McGuire, R. (2004). Stress: Keep things in perspective. Retrieved May 5, 2005, from http://www.pjonline.com/students/tp2004/p18stress.html

Transcripts

Task 2.4

Listen to the recording of some students reporting back on their discussion of the points listed in Task 2.1. Which of the statements do they refer to?

1

Student A: Our group thought the most controversial point was the first one – wanting to speak English with a native-speaker accent.

Presenter: **2**

Student B: Point 'd', concerning the importance of grammar and pronunciation, provoked the most discussion in our group. Some people felt that grammar was more important than pronunciation, but others disagreed strongly.

Presenter: **3**

Student A: Point 'f' was the most controversial point of discussion in our group; people were very divided over the issue of working in groups affecting their grammatical accuracy.

Presenter: **4**

Student B: There was some disagreement about point 'g', the point about speaking English for social reasons, but most of the group agreed that international students will need to communicate socially.

Presenter: **Task 3.2**

Now listen to the recording of two students discussing these statements. Does the second speaker agree, disagree or partly agree with each statement?

Presenter: **a)**

Speaker A: If you want to succeed at university, you really need to manage your time well.

Speaker B: Absolutely. I totally agree, because otherwise you will fall behind.

Presenter: **b)**

Speaker A: It's important to do a lot of reading around before you choose a focus for your essays.

Speaker B: Yes, that's true, but you need to limit the amount you read.

Presenter: **c)**

Speaker A: The best time to revise for exams is just before the exam, when the pressure is on.

Speaker B: I'm not sure I agree with you there. Many people can't think clearly under pressure.

Presenter:	**d)**	
Speaker A:	The same study skills are necessary on both undergraduate and postgraduate courses.	
Speaker B:	I agree up to a point, but postgraduates probably need more developed research skills.	
Presenter:	**e)**	
Speaker A:	If you've completed an academic course in one country, you should be able to cope with a course in another country.	
Speaker B:	Not necessarily. There are different academic cultures in different countries. You may have to learn a new approach to studying.	
Presenter:	**f)**	
Speaker A:	People have different learning styles. It helps you learn more quickly if you're aware of how you learn best.	
Speaker B:	That's a very good point. It can really help you to study more efficiently if you understand your own strengths and weaknesses.	
Presenter:	**Task 4.1**	
	Listen and number the points below according to the order in which the students discuss them.	
Sarah:	Hi Majid, how are you doing?	
Majid:	Yes, I am fine, and you Sarah?	
Sarah:	I'm fine, I haven't seen you in ages. How is your course going now?	
Majid:	It's just so much, to be honest. So much.	
Sarah:	Are you really busy?	
Majid:	Yes, really, really busy.	
Sarah:	I'm in my final year now and I have an awful lot of work on. I do History and it is so much reading.	
Majid:	Yes, it's the same, you know. I am doing Applied Linguistics and it is just beyond my head. It's so much reading.	
Sarah:	How do you cope with all the reading?	
Majid:	I try just to prioritise my reading lists. This is what I do. I read on a daily basis – I am not sure – as a native speaker maybe that is not your technique, is it?	
Sarah:	Well, being a native-speaking student I try to leave my reading to the last minute. But how do you pick out the relevant bits in your reading list? As a History student I get a list as long as my arm of different books to read by different people, and sometimes you don't know what's important. How do you do that?	
Majid:	I try just to focus on my lecture and after the lecture I ask my tutor which book would be very easy to read and give me a very good introduction about the topic. Otherwise I would just end up wasting my time searching for books that are relevant.	
Sarah:	Same here. I always try to speak to my tutor or my lecturer and ask them what is the best title to read. And also, because I do a subject where I have to write a lot of essays and a lot of analytical writing, I also try to ask them about who is on which side of the debate and who would give the best answer to a question.	

Majid: Yes, that is a very good idea. Do you mean that you try to ask your tutor about which book or what kind of writer each writer is, I mean try to understand the argument first?

Sarah: My course is an awful lot about different theories and different approaches to events that happened in the past and so it is very important when I look at my reading list to be able to see who said what about an event. So that helps a lot. But still it takes an awful lot of time.

Majid: Yes, and how do you manage your time?

Sarah: How do you, first?

Majid: I have to be honest because the reading is very difficult. I try to finish an article very quickly and follow the techniques that we learnt in the pre-sessional course, for example like skimming and scanning, and read the abstract first, things like this. And that is just to help me to cope with the time.

Sarah: I wish that they had taught us all these little handy hints and tips. As a native-speaking student they just expect you to know what to do.

Majid: Hmm!

Sarah: And, with, you know, trying to manage your time as well as all this reading, you've got all these essays and presentations to do throughout the term and sometimes you feel that you have got so much going on, there is an awful lot of stress. How do you manage stress?

Majid: It's very difficult this, a killer to be honest, and sometimes I just leave it and just have a chat with a friend or just relax sometimes, you know?

Sarah: With the university course, generally they are not very consistent. Some weeks you may have presentations and essays to do and some weeks you may have only a bit of reading. I find it helps to manage your time by, say, doing something before you have to do it, doing reading before you have to do it and also essays as well. Do you find that doing an essay early helps?

Majid: Yes, that's what I do. I start very early. I do a kind of a plan before I start my essay and then send it to my tutor and I ask him if it's a good plan or not and can I start writing in that topic if the plan is okay. And they usually give you very good feedback, and after the feedback I start reading and writing and try to finish very early. And when you finish your essays, how do you edit them well, what kinds of things do you do to them?

Sarah: When I write an essay, I try to write it in parts, but I don't know if this is a very good technique, it is just what I've done for many years. Once I have finished an essay, I read it and then I get someone else to read it, to make sure it makes sense and that it is not just made-up stuff in my head that doesn't make any sense at all. It is very important to have someone else read your work before you hand it in. Because especially in extended writing where it is your thoughts going down on paper it is very important that it makes sense.

Majid: Do you choose the topic that you are going to write about?

Sarah: Yes, it is very important when you choose any course that you are interested and want to do it. It must be even more important as a non-native speaker to be interested in what you are doing, so that you have the drive to keep going and persevere when things are hard.

Task 6.2

Listen to the recording of a student presenting his top five study tips. Are any of the points the same as yours?

Student: There are five main points which we consider important for successful study.

Our first point is you need to be well-organised. Without this, you will not be able to manage all the work you are given.

Next, we have put the importance of working with classmates. Students often need to cooperate with each other in seminars and planning presentations.

Moving onto our third point, keep good notes. There is so much information to deal with from both lectures and reading that you need to take notes effectively and reread these.

Fourthly, we think that good IT skills are now an essential part of university study. Students often need to use the Internet for research purposes, so they need to know how to search for useful information.

And finally, our last point is the importance of motivation – you really need to want to learn about your subject. If not, you will find it hard to study if you are just not interested in it.

Presenter: Unit 2: Learning online

Task 2.3

Now listen to a recording of a student comparing different perspectives on the statement in Task 2.1. What does the speaker say about the views of those involved?

Student: From a teacher's perspective, he or she would probably be concerned about the effect of the child's behaviour on other children – how it might negatively affect their progress and learning – so would probably want the child excluded from school.

From the point of view of the parents, they would say it was the teacher's and school's responsibility to deal with the child's behaviour problems and that excluding the child was an easy way out for the school. They would say that the child should remain and the school should work out a solution.

If I were the headteacher of the child's school, I'd probably feel that the reputation of the school might be damaged by excluding the child. It might give the school a bad name as people might think it was a problem school. As a headteacher, I'd want the child to remain at the school, despite the problems.

The child psychologist would argue that we need to understand and deal with the cause of the child's bad behaviour, and that excluding the child would not do that. In fact, it might damage the child more.

Presenter: **Task 4.1**

Listen to a student summarising a group discussion of the statement from Task 2.1 relating to the exclusion of disruptive children. Did the group agree or disagree with the statement?

Student: This is a difficult question, but we finally all agreed that such a child should be excluded from school, as this would be in the best interests of most people concerned. It's true that this action might cause some damage to the child's long-term ability to socialise effectively with other children, so we also agreed that this action should only be taken if there is no other solution, I mean, if all else fails.

Presenter: **Task 4.5**

Listen to the recording of a student using the phrases. Practise saying them in a way that is natural.

Student: After much consideration, we decided that corporal punishment is not really necessary to maintain discipline in schools.

All things considered, we felt that children should not leave school until they are 18.

On balance, we felt that parents should not be allowed to educate their children at home.

We couldn't reach agreement on this issue. Some of us felt that corporal punishment is necessary, whilst others disagreed strongly.

We recognised that there are some disadvantages for the child, such as pressure and stress, but we still felt exams at a young age are a good idea.

We're fully aware that lack of discipline in schools is a major problem. However, we still felt that corporal punishment is not the answer.

One has to acknowledge that some parents could educate their children very well. We still felt, however, that only parents with teaching qualifications should be allowed to do this by law.

So, although we agreed with the statement, we stressed that children of 15 should receive careful advice on which subjects to choose.

Presenter: Unit 3: Changing roles in the family

Task 3.3

Listen to a student presenting key points from the same article. Refer to OHT 2 as you listen.

Student: As the title suggests, this article deals with an apparent change in the role men would like to play in family life. First of all, it provides some statistics to support this claim, then looks at two issues related to it: the decline in the social stigma attached to being a stay-at-home dad and the question of the resources needed to support men who choose this new role. 5

So, the article reports that increasing numbers of men would prefer to stop working or work less in order to look after their children and home. It refers to statistics from the government, which show that 155,000 men now stay at home full-time to look after their children. Of these, 60 per cent do so voluntarily; it is their choice. I presume the other 40 per cent do so because they are unemployed and have no choice. 10

The article also gives statistics from a magazine survey of 2,000 couples. As you can see, only one-third of those asked, 34 per cent in fact, wanted to continue working full-time after having children. The majority either wanted to return to part-time work or become full-time househusbands. This is what the men in the poll said they wanted. According to the article, however, what stops them from actually giving up 15 work and staying at home is, not surprisingly, money or worries about money.

The article then goes on to say that the social stigma attached to men stopping work to bring up a family is disappearing … social stigma – this means something people might be ashamed of doing, that society would not approve of. As I said, this is disappearing, so you now see more men coming in to schools and playgroups 20 to collect their children.

Finally, the article argues that more resources are needed to support these new full-time fathers, such as this website www.homedad.org. It quotes a founder of the website as saying that most current resources for parents are aimed at mothers. So, the article reports on some interesting changes in social attitudes to work and fatherhood. However, it doesn't mention the effect of socioeconomic background on men's decisions or wishes regarding work and parenthood. I mean, the men who are choosing or wanting to give up work to become househusbands, are these men from high, middle or lower income groups? We don't know this from the text, but this could be significant data. 25 30

Presenter:	**Task 3.5**
	Now listen to these three extracts. Underline where the speaker slows down and stresses particular words or phrases.
	Extract 1
Student:	The article also gives statistics from a magazine survey of 2,000 couples. As you can see, only one-third of those asked, 34 per cent in fact, wanted to continue working full-time after having children. The majority either wanted to return to part-time work or become full-time househusbands.
Presenter:	**Extract 2**
Student:	The article then goes on to say that the social stigma attached to men stopping work to bring up a family is disappearing ... social stigma – this means something people might be ashamed of doing, that society would not approve of. As I said, this is disappearing, so you now see more men coming to schools and playgroups to collect their children.
Presenter:	**Extract 3**
Student:	So, the article reports on some interesting changes in social attitudes to work and fatherhood. However, it doesn't mention the effect of socioeconomic background on men's decisions or wishes regarding work and parenthood. I mean, the men who are choosing or wanting to give up work to become househusbands, are these men from high, middle or lower income groups?
Presenter:	**Task 5.4**
	Listen to the recording of students exchanging opinions on different topics. Tick the expressions you hear.
	1
Student A:	It seems to me that women are being forced to have careers when they really want to stay at home.
Student B:	I take your point, but don't you think that's making an assumption that all women want to have children?
Presenter:	**2**
Student A:	In my view, women are biologically designed to bring up children, and men to be the breadwinners.
Student B:	Well, I think that is a rather old-fashioned idea.
Presenter:	**3**
Student A:	Just because it's traditional or normal for women to stay at home, doesn't necessarily mean it's natural.

Student B:	I understand what you're saying, but you have to consider this question from the perspective of different cultures.
Presenter:	**4**
Student A:	Women are built differently, and are not suitable for certain jobs, such as engineering and construction.
Student B:	Well, I'm not sure if that's quite true – you need to consider the reality, that in fact a number of women are employed in the construction industry.
Presenter:	Unit 4: A healthy lifestyle

Task 4.2

Listen to the recording of these expressions in context. Tick the ones which you hear.

1

Student A:	It's not really up to the government to do something about smoking, is it? Why do we always expect the government to deal with these sorts of issues, rather than making smokers themselves face up to the problem?
Student B:	So what you're saying is that there is no point in the government trying to tackle the problem of smoking until individuals take responsibility for their own health …
Presenter:	**2**
Student A:	I don't see why this subject gets so much attention. People have always had to work hard and I'm sure it will continue like that. If you're organised, it shouldn't be a problem.
Student B:	So in your view, dealing with stress is not a major issue; people just need to manage their time properly …
Presenter:	**3**
Student A:	So as far as I am concerned, it needs to be approached from the perspective of having a healthy and happy lifestyle … do you understand what I mean?
Student B:	Yes, absolutely.
Presenter:	**4**
Student A:	The fast food industry is only concerned with making a profit. It will mislead the public about what's in the junk food they sell. It can't be left to police itself.
Student B:	I'm not sure I understand what you mean.
Student A:	What I'm saying is that the fast food industry is not concerned about people's health. They just want to make money, so they won't tell the truth about what they put in hamburgers, for example. The government needs to pass laws controlling what can be put in junk food. You can't just leave it to the fast food industry to decide.
Presenter:	Unit 5: The influence of the media

Task 3.2

Listen to the description of the data shown. What details does the speaker highlight? What point is the speaker making by showing this data?

Speaker: This graph shows monthly visits to the cinema by age groups between 1984 and 2003.

As you can see, young people aged between 15 and 24 are the most likely age group to go to the cinema. Fifty-four per cent of this age group attended the cinema once a month or more in Great Britain in 2003. In 2003, 39 per cent of children aged seven to 14 went to the cinema once a month or more, as can be seen from this line here. The percentage for both these age groups has risen noticeably since 1984.

From this data, it is clear that going to the cinema is still a popular form of entertainment, despite the arrival of videos, DVDs and computer games.

Presenter: **Task 3.3**

Listen to the recording again and fill in the gaps in the excerpt.
[REPEAT OF TASK 3.2]

Presenter: **Task 4.1**

You are going to hear a journalist talking about the BBC.

Interviewer: So Paul, can you tell us a little bit about how the BBC got started initially?

BBC employee: The BBC was set up in 1922. Um, its first director general was a 33-year-old Scottish engineer called John Reith, who was invited to become the first director and his vision, it is important to know this guy's name, John Reith, his vision was very important for the establishing of the BBC. His vision of what it should be was very, very influential. Um, basically he had a phrase which he used which was to inform, educate and entertain. And this was the three pilllars of what he thought the BBC should do.

Interviewer: Mmm.

BBC employee: Inform, educate and entertain, in that order. It is interesting that educate comes before entertain.

Interviewer: Indeed, yes.

BBC employee: Yes, in his vision of it, and this kind of motto is still used in the BBC today, inform, educate and entertain, and it can still be seen in something that is called the Reith Lectures that happen every year. Radio lectures on an important scientific or cultural issue of the day which are dedicated to Lord Reith, the first director general.

Interviewer: And was it accepted from very early on that the BBC would be an independent organisation editorially?

BBC employee: Yes, um, that is very interesting, um, John Reith's vision was that the BBC should be financially independent and editorially independent. Financially, well he had seen the commercial radio being set up in the USA and commercial radio was basically paid for by the advertising. So the advertisers had a lot of power and he had seen other European broadcasters being set up, who were controlled by the government, and so there was a lot of political influence over them. And he wanted something that would be completely separate from both of them, and that was his vision.

He was tested very early on, actually, in 1926, only four years after the BBC was set up there was the General Strike. This took place during the Great Depression of the 20s and everybody was on strike. Newspapers weren't being printed, people couldn't get information and the Home Secretary at the time, Mr Winston Churchill, tried to use the BBC to broadcast government propaganda. But John Reith was very, very strict about this, absolutely refused to broadcast what he saw as government propaganda and tried to broadcast independently what the BBC thought was

Interviewer: actually happening, and I guess this was the beginning of the BBC's reputation for total independence in its news reporting.

Interviewer: Yes, I mean one of the most admirable qualities of the BBC has been its ability to maintain its independence and, um, I am wondering if this has been challenged in various, if it is still being challenged over this.

BBC employee: The BBC's political independence has been challenged constantly over its history, really. Especially in the last twenty years, it has been attacked by both right-wing and left-wing political parties. In the 1980s, Margaret Thatcher and the Conservative Party used to call it the Bolshevik Broadcasting Company. Bolshevik as in the Russian Revolution, they claimed it was very biased and very left-wing. And recently the left-wing party, the Labour Party, have had a very serious falling out with the BBC over the Iraq war. What became known as the Kelly Affair. Basically the BBC claimed in a radio programme that the government had deliberately exaggerated the threat from Saddam Hussein's Iraq in order to persuade the public to go to war with Iraq. The government denied that they had been misleading the public. They were very angry about the BBC's report and the scientist at the centre of this big argument, who had actually given the information to the BBC, unfortunately committed suicide, and there was a great big argument, big public investigation about this, and in the end the judge who was leading the investigation, decided for the government and against the BBC, and the BBC had to apologise and the leader, actually the director general at the time actually, resigned, although a lot of the general public didn't agree with this ruling.

Interviewer: Absolutely, yes.

BBC employee: It was a very serious setback for the BBC.

Interviewer: Yes, and it was very evident in the march to London when one million people took to the streets to demonstrate against the government.

BBC employee: Certainly, yeah, and that had to be reported just by the BBC just as much as the propaganda for going to war with Iraq was reported, and they both had to be reported in a balanced way.

Interviewer: Yes, so in many ways the BBC has been a very controversial organisation throughout the ages since it started.

BBC employee: It certainly has.

Interviewer: I am wondering how it manages to finance itself throughout all of this.

BBC employee: Well, the BBC has a special, I think unique, form of financing at the moment, where it gets money from people, from everybody who has a TV. If you have a TV in your house you must pay a licence for it every year, and that includes students. That might be some of your students might need to get one. The licences are £121, I think, and …

Interviewer: Quite a substantial amount!

BBC Employee: Quite a substantial amount, which you have to pay every year and this money is used for making radio and TV programmes. The BBC has other ways of making money and it sells its programmes abroad to other channels, it makes books which tie in with its programmes and it has various merchandising branches, but it doesn't carry advertising. The only advertising you will see on the BBC is for other BBC programmes.

Interviewer: Yes, yes. And it is one of the reasons why people opt to watch BBC rather than other channels.

BBC employee: Some people find it very refreshing not to have to have advertisements every 15 minutes.

Interviewer: Yes, especially in the middle of films.

And the BBC still does continue to play a very important role in people's lives. Very often at lunchtime, breaktime, you will hear people talking about a progamme that they had seen on television.

BBC employee: Yes, BBC plays an integral part in British life. People have grown up with it for generations. There are soap operas on BBC radio which are 50 years old. It is the oldest soap opera in the world. It is the nation's favourite information source. Most people still get their information from the BBC. The BBC is still the most trusted organisation in the country.

Interviewer: So why do you think the BBC still plays such an important role in British life? I mean, very often at lunchtime, the topic of conversation would be a programme that people have watched the night before.

BBC employee: Absolutely, I think the BBC still plays an integral part in British life. People have grown up with it for generations. It is like a trusted friend. It is still where people get most of their information from. Certainly, the BBC is more trusted than any politician and people are very protective of it. They don't like to see the BBC being attacked by politicians. I also think people are very proud of the BBC. They see broadcasting as something that we still do well in this country. The BBC itself still claims that it is the second most recognised brand name in the world, after Coca-Cola.

Interviewer: *[laughs]* And it certainly offers us a lot more than Coca-Cola does! Thank you very much, Paul.

BBC employee: Thank you

Interviewer: Very informative.

Presenter: **Task 5.3**

Listen to three students discussing freedom of speech.

Student A: I don't think you can really put any limits on freedom of speech. It should be an absolute principle in a mature democracy, don't you think?

Student B: When you say "an absolute principle", do you mean that anyone can say or broadcast or print anything they want to about anyone else on any subject?

Student A: Yes, I think so. Obviously, you expect that people will use that right responsibly and not use it in a way that will lead to violence or worse.

Student C: Yes, I think I agree. I mean, once you start putting limits on freedom of speech, then it's a dangerous road to go down. As you said, it's a fundamental part of a democratic society. If those in authority start restricting that right, if those in power have the right to decide what can or can't be said, then I think it's a dangerous sort of power to have. You made an interesting point about using the right to freedom of speech in a responsible way. That's what I think a mature democracy should be based on – people have the right to free speech, but are responsible enough not to abuse it, not to exercise it in a negative way.

Student B: Yes, but following on from that point, that's where I have a problem with the idea of an absolute right to freedom of speech, particularly regarding what you both say about responsibility and mature democracies. The reality is people can't be trusted to use that right in a responsible way. Why should people have the right to make racist comments or things which might cause violence against others or whatever? Can I also pick up on your point about not allowing those in power to limit freedom of speech? I mean, I would have thought that in a mature democracy, yes, those in power must listen to the majority, but they also need to protect minorities, and that means limiting the rights of people to say things in public which might put those minority groups in danger.

Student A: OK, those are fair arguments, but you make the point that a society needs to protect minority groups, but if the government can limit freedom of speech, they might start silencing minority groups and that's not protecting them. There might be less tolerance of different, non-majority views and opinions.

Student C: Exactly.

Student B: I know, it's not an easy question, but I still think that a society in which anyone can say anything may in fact lead to a less tolerant society than one where there are some limits on what you can say. As I said before, people might use free speech to take away the freedom of other people to feel safe in a society.

Student C: I think we'll have to agree to disagree on this issue.

Presenter: Unit 7: The world of work

Task 4.5

Listen to the interview. Take notes of Sonia's replies to the questions. Is there any information from the interview you might be able to use in your discussion?

Interviewer: Good morning, Sonia. You've done some research into the role of women in the construction industry specifically. Can I start, however, by asking you about the participation of women in the labour market more generally? What are the reasons why more women are participating in the labour market?

Sonia Gurjao: The main reasons for women's increased participation in the labour market would be the deskilling of historically male jobs. Secondly, demographics have changed. We have an increased life expectancy and women today tend to have fewer children than they did in the past. We also have a restructuring of psychological expectations, such as women's own expectations of themselves and what they want to do in life and today, in today's day and age, it's become an economic necessity to have two incomes in a family to be able to support a family and to be able to accommodate the general running of the house.

Interviewer: Is that because of the cost of living?

Sonia Gurjao: Yes, that is because of the increased cost of living today. And another reason is women are more highly educated today than they have ever been in the past. And all these factors contribute towards their increased participation in the labour market.

Interviewer: Now, moving on to the construction industry itself. Is the construction industry a common career choice for women?

Sonia Gurjao: No, actually, the construction industry is not an obvious career choice for women. In fact, lots of women are not informed about the construction industry as a career of choice. This starts right from schools, where they aren't informed of construction, science, engineering and technology subjects as a choice that they could do or pursue as their career choices. And one of the reasons is the construction industry also has a bad image, that is one related to hard work, and working in extreme conditions. It's known as the dirty industry and it's not attractive to women as such.

Interviewer: As I understand it, from your research, the construction industry does need more women though to join it? Why is that?

Sonia Gurjao: The construction industry plays a critical role in Britain's prosperity and it employs over two million people, and in the past it had a steady choice of entrants into the industry, probably because of the way people chose their careers and people pursued vocational training, but with the change in the education system and people pursuing higher education, the traditional source of labour doesn't tend to go into vocational training and so we now see a skills shortage in the construction industry. And with 50 per cent of the labour participation being women, today for the construction industry, including women within construction becomes a very important aspect.

Interviewer: Has the construction industry itself made any attempts to try to recruit women into the industry?

Sonia Gurjao: The construction industry has not actively gone into recruiting women, but as they've seen, and as the government's seen that there's going to be a problem with recruiting your traditional force of labour, they've started looking into recruiting women as a solution to the labour problems and also making the construction industry more inclusive and looking for talent from the other 50 per cent of the labour workforce. So, what they've done is they've gone to schools and they have projects where they encourage young girls to do, like they have little training sessions and they have workshops where they actively participate and build things to encourage them or to show them what working in the construction industry might be like.

Interviewer: So, they've gone to the schools ...

Sonia Gurjao: They've started from school levels and then they have, even for young people, they've started for career advisors, they've started training career advisors into encouraging or to stop stereotyping career choices for young people.

Interviewer: And that's to try and encourage young girls ...

Sonia Gurjao: Not just young girls, but to also encourage boys as well into construction. Because it's not only girls who lack interest in the construction industry, it is also the lack of men in the construction industry.

Interviewer: I understand that the industry has a problem with keeping women who join the construction industry. Why is that and is there a solution to this problem?

Sonia Gurjao: I think that's a recent realisation from the part of the industry. They have a long-working-hour culture because of the kind of projects there are, because they tend to be projects that need to be deadlines, because of the cost involved in the projects as well. So, ultimately what happens is when you have women who are 50 per cent of the workforce, but then out of these 50 per cent of the workforce, around 44 per cent of women actually only work part-time and the industry doesn't have part-time working, so that makes it difficult for women to be present in the industry, to be working. So that's where the industry has started realising that if we have to recruit women we have to make an attempt to be flexible, as in other industries like telecommunications and banking, which have of course benefited from making their jobs flexible.

Interviewer: Could you just summarise what you see to be the main barriers which women face today in joining or staying in the construction industry?

Sonia Gurjao: What we repeatedly hear in the past is that the construction industry is dirty, dangerous and not suitable for women. But in today's day and age, where technology has taken over and we have more managing of projects and we have consultancy, so in today's construction industry, the main barriers would actually be flexible working in terms of 44 per cent of women actually working part-time in the labour force participation. If we need to target that, we need to make the industry more flexible and it needs to see that people need to have a better work/life balance and organisations need to change to accommodate this.

Presenter: Unit 8: Protecting the environment

Task 4.2

Listen to a recording of a student using *Useful language* expressions from Task 1. Underline the words or phrases from the box which the speaker uses.

1 Most of the respondents claimed that they take recycling seriously and recycled glass, plastic and paper products.

2 Approximately a third of those interviewed were prepared to be part of a car-sharing scheme.

3 Just over 50 per cent of the subjects said that they would buy environmentally-friendly products even if those products were more expensive.

Presenter: Unit 10: Studying in a new environment

Task 3.1

Listen to a speaker who recently completed a postgraduate degree at a British university. Take notes on the advice given by the speaker, so that afterwards you will be able to explain it to someone who has not listened to it.

Text 1

EAP tutor: Hello, Gulin. Thanks for agreeing to come and talk about the experience of studying here as an international student. You're just finishing a one-year Masters course, aren't you?

Gulin: Yes, that's right.

EAP tutor: What has it been like for you, working with British and other international students together?

Gulin: Well, it has been a new kind of experience for me. Everything was new to me at the beginning. But as in any new situation, I gradually learnt to adapt. I think that, if you're studying at a university with people from all over the world, you need to accept that there will be cultural differences between people and you need to be tolerant of them so that you can get along with people well enough to work with them. Oh, and of course, it's right to expect other people to show a similar acceptance and tolerance towards you.

EAP tutor: Yes, I know that students are sometimes advised to form study groups with others on the course. Did you do that, and, if so, was it helpful?

Gulin: Yes, I agree that's a good idea. But of course it doesn't work with just anybody. I think it's worth looking for people who have similar study habits to your own, and if possible people who don't live too far away from you. And, again, you have to be prepared to be flexible; to adjust your own approach a little sometimes, so that it's easier for the other people to work with you.

EAP tutor: Now, what about the tutor? When you started your course, was it clear to you how to approach the tutor and what for?

Gulin: I think the responsibilities of the tutor are written in the department's handbook.

EAP tutor: That's good.

Gulin: So the student should read that to get a basic idea of the support she is entitled to expect from her tutor. But you need to play it by ear a little at first, because obviously tutors are human and so they are different. You have to approach different tutors in different ways. One point I would make about meetings with your tutor is: it is worth preparing a little bit before the meeting – working out the questions you want to ask and the kind of answers you expect or need, so that you make the best possible use of the time during the meeting. Personally, I take in a list of points in order of priority: like 1, 2, 3, 4, etc.

EAP tutor: Apart from your tutor and fellow students, what other resources have you made use of during your period of study?

Gulin: Well, I would advise any new student to explore the university campus early on in her stay, if possible with some guidance from a more experienced student to get to know the facilities that are available. The first place I explored was the library – it's important to find which parts of the library are particularly relevant to your subject area, and to discover whether there are other, specialist libraries or collections in some departments. For example, in my case, there were books on linguistics in one part of the main library, periodicals in the other part, and then there was the departmental library and also a useful library in a neighbouring college. It took a while to discover where everything was.

But the library is not the only facility which is open to all students: some departments or units run an advisory service. This means that at certain times of the day students from any department can go along and ask for help with their project. It's well worthwhile asking about the advisory services early on in your course, and don't be afraid to make use of them – they are there to help students, that's their function.

EAP tutor: Did you use these advisory services yourself?

Gulin: Oh, yes, two of them. The advisory service in the Computer Centre has helped me several times: once when my disk was stuck, and another time when I thought I'd lost a lot of data … And the Applied Statistics Department also runs an advisory service, which I would recommend to anyone who is going to do experimental research. The staff there will discuss the design of the experiment with you – of course, you should do this early on in your project at the planning stage, so that it's not too late to make any changes that they suggest. They will also help you analyse the data later on.

EAP tutor: Right. The facilities you've mentioned so far have been broadly academic. What other kinds would you advise new students to make use of?

Gulin: They should make use of the Students' Union, of course; after all, it is supposed to be run by the students for the students. It has an Overseas Students Committee, which is made up of people who have already been in the UK for a year or two and want to use their experience to improve the services provided for overseas students. You can contact them at the Students' Union.

Another good reason for visiting the Union, as well as the shops, is that it's the information centre for the various university clubs or groups, and for student activities in general. In one part of the building there are several big notice boards, where groups can advertise forthcoming events and sometimes a list for people to sign up if they are interested in a particular activity. There are also boards for other kinds of notice: for example, people who want to share accommodation, or second-hand books for sale.

EAP tutor: I imagine those groups are a good way for overseas students to meet British students, for social reasons and also perhaps to practise speaking English.

Gulin: Yes, I agree.

EAP tutor: Did you do that yourself? Did you join one of these clubs?

Gulin: Oh yes, I joined the Chess Club. That was a good move, because sometimes you need a place where you can get right away from your academic studies for a while. Chess is always refreshing; you sit down and … I guess you use a different part of the brain. And as well as the chess itself, there is the social contact. People tend to talk a lot at our chess evenings; maybe not so much during, but before and after their games; not just about chess – all kinds of things.

EAP tutor: And what about sports? I know there are quite a lot of sports clubs advertised on the notice boards as well.

Gulin: Yes, there are various sports, and the one I'm interested in is mountaineering …

EAP tutor: Mountaineering!

Gulin: Yes. It can be quite demanding, but it gives you a sense of satisfaction when you climb … the highest mountain in Wales, for example.

EAP tutor: I'll have to take your word for that. Right, finally, is there any advice that you wish you'd had at the beginning of your course?

Gulin: Yes, to be prepared for a style of lecture in which contributions from the audience are often invited by the lecturer. If you are not used to this style, it can at first seem off-putting, even aggressive. Try to practise contributing so that you can join in the discussion.

Perhaps I should explain that, although contributions to the class discussion were encouraged, it was certainly not acceptable for a student to engage in private discussion with the one or two people nearest to him during a lecture. That happened a couple of times in the first week of my course, and it was an irritating distraction for the lecturer and all the other students.

One final point: make an effort to see the course as a whole from the start. If, as in my case, the most important part of the course in terms of both assessment and learning is a dissertation project, use the early parts of the course to prepare for the dissertation. Jot down ideas about it from time to time, to help you gradually work towards it.

EAP tutor: Right, well, thank you very much, Gulin. You've been very helpful.

Gulin: It was a pleasure.

Presenter: **Text 2**

EAP tutor: Now, Chris, can I get this right? You've just completed an MSc course on which a large proportion of the students were international students? Is that right?

Chris: That's it. Yes, I was in AERD – that's the Department of Agricultural Extension and Rural Development.

EAP tutor: And how do you think the students from other countries got on on that course?

Chris: Pretty well. I think we found as the course went on that we were all in the same boat really. For example, the majority of both home and international students were returning to full-time study after several years in work. That was an important thing to have in common.

EAP tutor: What advice would you give students, particularly international students, based on your experience as a student here?

Chris: I think the most basic thing is to make use, full use, of your tutors and lecturers. Maybe some of the overseas students, perhaps even some of the home students, don't do that. They're a bit too shy early on of taking questions or problems to tutors or of making use of the time that tutors make available. So, the first piece of advice I'd give, I think, is to find out at the beginning of your course the times at which your tutor is going to be available for tutorial appointments, and then make full use of them.

EAP tutor: So, any problems, they should tell the tutor as soon as possible?

Chris: Yes.

EAP tutor: And, of course, if they're in a department where they don't have a personal tutor, I suppose they could go to the lecturer concerned. Moving on, what about the amount of reading that you have to do as a university student?

Chris: Yes! It looked pretty daunting at first, with those long reading lists. I think the important point here is to be selective: don't think you have to read everything that's listed – you're not expected to. Find which are the most important items on the list – ask the lecturer or tutor if necessary, and then, if your time is limited, spend it reading those books thoroughly.

EAP tutor: What about study resources on the campus – the library, for example. Any tips there?

Chris: Yes, make use of the recall system. If, when you get to the library, you find that the particular books you need have been borrowed by someone else, don't give up. Fill out a recall slip, hand it in at the information desk, and within a few days the library will contact you to tell you the book is now ready to collect. Once I discovered this system, unfortunately not until halfway through my course, I used it a lot and I found it very helpful. Of course, it means you need to plan your work properly; it's no good leaving the essential reading for an assignment until just before the deadline, and then trying to use the recall system – it's too late then.

EAP tutor: Any advice on working with other students?

Chris: When you are given an assignment, definitely talk to your fellow students about it: discuss your initial ideas about it, and then later how you're getting on with it, what you're finding difficult, etc. This will help you to think around the topic, and will also reassure you that you are not the only person feeling the strain.

And if you feel keen, you can try setting up a study group with some of the others. On our course, for example, five of us formed a study group in the second term and worked together on revising for the exams. But a study group can be helpful at any point in the course – for a particular assignment, for instance. You need to work out which of the other students on your course you find it easy to work with, maybe people who have the same approach to study as you, or simply people who live in the same hall of residence as you. I got together with four others and we decided that we could do the reading for the exams more enjoyably and more efficiently by sharing it. So we agreed which person should read which item on the list, and then we met up once or twice a week after lectures and summarised our reading for each other. And when someone wasn't clear about something, or disagreed with something, we discussed it. I learnt a lot from that. It also made me more confident about expressing my ideas, as you need to do in seminars.

EAP tutor: So, try to form a study group with other students to share the workload.

Chris: Yes.

EAP tutor: Now, what about choosing options? That's often a very important part of a course, making selections about exactly what you will study. Any advice there?

Chris: One point I would make is, perhaps it's obvious: choose options according to which subject interests you, not according to who the lecturer is. Don't choose an option simply because it's organised by someone who gives nice, clear lectures. There may be a greater risk of some overseas students making this mistake because they are so concerned about understanding every word of a lecture. But we all agreed, at the end of our course, that the subject, not the lecturer, should be the most important consideration when you choose options. If you choose a subject that really interests you, it is quite likely to provide you with a dissertation topic that you are really motivated to work on.

EAP tutor: Right, well that's …

Chris: So, go for the subject not the lecturer.

EAP tutor: That's my next question, actually! Any advice on writing the dissertation – if you're a postgraduate – or an extended essay if you're an undergraduate?

Chris: As soon as you have drafted a proposal, an outline of what you intend to write about, have a meeting with your tutor or supervisor to establish whether the basic idea is viable. This is important because otherwise you might spend days working on a project, only to discover at a later stage that a supervisor has some basic objection to what you're doing, and you have wasted a lot of time. So, have an early meeting to get some official feedback on your proposal.

One other point about working on a major project, such as a dissertation: draw up a work schedule at the beginning, with reasonable deadlines by which you intend to complete each stage of the project. The project can seem like a huge mountain to climb at first, so it's good for morale if you divide it up into manageable sections: 'I'll finish reading by the end of April, I'll complete data collection by mid-May, and then I'll write the first two chapters by the end of May'; that kind of thing. Even if you don't meet all the deadlines, you will have a sense of progress.

EAP tutor: OK, that's very helpful, Chris. Thank you very much.

Chris: No, not at all.

Appendix 1: Signpost expressions for presentations

Introducing the presentation

Good morning/afternoon, ladies and gentlemen …

The topic of my presentation today is …

Today I am going to talk about …

If you have any questions, I would be happy to answer these at the end of the presentation.

Giving an overview of the presentation

This presentation will deal with three main points …

My presentation is divided into three main sections …

First of all I will … then I will move on to examine … and finally …

Transition expressions

Moving on to the next point, …

Now I'd like to look at …

The third area which needs to be considered is …

And finally, my last point is …

Referring to visual aids

As you can see …

From this chart/table/graph, it is clear that …

This graph/table/chart shows …

Concluding the presentation

Finally, …

To sum up, …

As this presentation has clearly shown, it is essential that …

Thank you for your attention … are there any questions?

Appendix 2: Sample OHTs

OHT 1

Men want to be househusbands

Now acceptable for men, not women, to be at home
155,000 men at home full-time, 60 per cent voluntarily
– Government statistics (2001)

More men are working part-time or flexi-hours in order
to take on the job of chief carer.

After they become fathers:
one-third: wanted to continue in full-time work
one-third: preferred to go part-time
one-third: preferred to become stay-at-home fathers

The only thing keeping them from staying at home is
money – the biggest concern for most prospective fathers,
who said financial fears cause them more anxiety than
worries about their loss of freedom.

Less social stigma for househusbands – now socially
acceptable to be a househusband. There are many more
fathers to be seen at playgroups and schools, dropping
off and picking up, in between running the family home.

Website now set up for dads to support each other in
childraising. Only UK support group helping dads who
are staying at home.

Men want to be househusbands

More men want to stay at home and look after children

- 155,000 men now at home full-time

- 60% voluntarily

(Government statistics 2001)

Only 34 per cent of fathers want to stay in full-time work

- Most fathers want to go part-time or stop work

- Main problem: financial worries

(*Pregnancy and Birth* magazine – poll of 2,000 couples)

Less social stigma for househusbands

- Fathers more present at school, playgroups, etc.

Lack of resources for stay-at-homes dads

e.g., www.homedad.org.uk

Appendix 3: Preparing and planning a presentation

There are many aspects of a good presentation and, during the course, you have worked on some of these aspects. For example,

- delivery (p11)
- what to include in a PowerPoint slide (p12)
- thinking of your audience concerning content and what needs to be explained (p23)

In some cases, you were giving a short presentation about a topic in order to lead into a discussion. In other cases, you were presenting information, a summary of a text or programme. However, in future situations you may be giving a presentation based on your own work or research, and you will need to spend a lot of time working on the content and organisation of the presentation. Below is a list of stages you may find helpful.

Stage 1: Find out what you need to do

1 Make sure you know exactly what the topic is or, if you are choosing your own topic, what is expected of you.

2 Check the length of time you have for the presentation.

3 Think about your audience – how much are they likely to know about the topic/how much will you need to explain?

4 If the presentation is being assessed, make sure you know what the criteria are.

Stage 2: Brainstorm ideas

5 Make a list of anything you can think of related to your topic; you will not use all of these ideas, but will choose from them afterwards.

6 Look at your list of ideas – what connections can you see between them? Are there particular ideas you could develop that would be of interest to your audience?

7 Decide which ideas to use – can each one be summarised in one sentence? If not, perhaps your ideas are not clear and specific enough.

8 Explain your ideas to a friend – this will help you to clarify them.

Stage 3: Do any necessary research

9 Determine if there are any ideas you need to get more information about.

10 Gather any evidence you need to support your ideas, e.g., statistics.

11 Think about how much information you can realistically convey to your audience.

12 Keep your audience in mind, especially in relation to their level of expertise.

Stage 4: Organise your ideas

13 Decide which point you should begin with.

14 Think about how you can link one idea to the next.

15 Do not include too much information – you want your audience to understand your key points clearly.

16 Decide how you will begin and end your presentation. In the introduction you want to get the attention of the audience. The conclusion is the last part of your presentation, and probably what the audience will most remember.

17 Prepare your PowerPoint slides – remember: 'less is more'.

18 Think of the key words you will use and check your pronunciation with a native speaker – there is nothing worse than listening to a presentation where the presenter pronounces the title of the presentation incorrectly!

Stage 5: Practise ...

19 to make sure you know your content well.

20 to check the time of the presentation.

22 to develop your confidence.

23 to anticipate some of the questions people might ask.

24 to make sure that your presentation does justice to all the hard work you have put into preparing it.

Appendix 4: Possible topics for seminar discussions

Congestion charging is the most effective means of preventing traffic congestion.

Banning smoking in public places contravenes human rights.

Women should play the same role as men in the armed forces.

Free education is an impractical dream.

People should not be allowed to …

GM food is the best means of solving global shortages.

Globalisation is only a threat to a small minority of individual cultures.

Sport should play a far greater role in school curricula.

The advance of information technology is creating a less sociable society.

The development of free markets is the most effective way of solving the world's economic problems.

Career Drivers Questionnaire

What are your drivers? How do they influence your career? Complete the questionnaire below to help you assess your own career drivers.

There are no right and wrong answers. You have a total of 50 points. Allocate ten points – no more, no less, between the nine items in each of the five sections. If you wish, you may allocate ten points to one item if the other items in the section are of no importance to you.

SECTION ONE

These things are important to me:

1. ☐ I seek a high standard of living.
2. ☐ I wish to influence others.
3. ☐ I only feel satisfied if the output from my job has real value in itself.
4. ☐ I want to be an expert in the things I do.
5. ☐ I seek to be creative at work.
6. ☐ I strive to work only with people I like.
7. ☐ I choose jobs where I am 'my own boss'.
8. ☐ I take steps to be 100% financially secure.
9. ☐ I want to acquire a social status that other people will respect.

SECTION TWO

In my working life I want to:

10. ☐ become an expert in a chosen field.
11. ☐ build close relationships with others at work.
12. ☐ become a leader in teams and organisations.
13. ☐ be part of 'the establishment'.
14. ☐ take decisions that I really believe in.
15. ☐ get the highest paid jobs.
16. ☐ have a job with long-term security.
17. ☐ take my own decisions about how I spend my time at work.
18. ☐ create things that people associate with me alone.

Source: © Garrat, B. & Frances, D. (1994) Managing your Own Career, HarperCollins Publisher Ltd.

SECTION THREE

If I am considering a new career opportunity:

19. ☐ I am drawn to roles with high social status.
20. ☐ I wish to be seen as a real specialist in my field.
21. ☐ I want to work to make a contribution to the wider community.
22. ☐ I want to look ahead at life and feel that I will always be okay.
23. ☐ I seek influence over others.
24. ☐ I wish to build warm personal relationships with people at work.
25. ☐ I want a high standard of living.
26. ☐ I want a degree of control over my own job.
27. ☐ Producing things that bear my name attract me.

SECTION FOUR

I would be disappointed if:

28. ☐ my work was not part of my 'search for meaning' in life.
29. ☐ I did not practise highly skilled work.
30. ☐ I could not afford a high standard of living.
31. ☐ my job gave no opportunity to create something new or different.
32. ☐ I did not know where I would stand on retirement day.
33. ☐ I worked without friends.
34. ☐ I did not receive recognition or honours.
35. ☐ I had to refer to others for decisions.
36. ☐ I wasn't in charge of people.

SECTION FIVE

A 'good' job means to me:

37. ☐ avoiding being a cog in a big wheel.
38. ☐ an excellent income.
39. ☐ plenty of time to study specialist subjects.
40. ☐ being a person who takes important decisions.
41. ☐ producing products or services that have my name on them.
42. ☐ having good relationships with other people.
43. ☐ being 'in charge' of others.
44. ☐ being secure.
45. ☐ doing what I believe is important.

Appendix 6: Sample proposal

Title:
A study of the correlation between students' understanding of the concepts of critical thinking, and their performance in synthesising sources into an academic text.

Rationale for the study:
International students find great difficulty in effectively incorporating material from a range of sources. There are a number of key factors which influence this ability, one of which is obviously linguistic ability. Another less tangible factor is that of understanding the conventions of critical thinking, as understood in British academic studies.

This research will attempt to identify students' perceptions of critical thinking and their knowledge of the concept. It will then attempt to analyse if there is a correlation between this understanding and the ability to read, analyse and synthesise information.

Proposed research questions:
Is there a correlation between students' understanding of the process of critical thinking and their ability to select materials appropriately and incorporate these into their written work?

Do students of different cultural backgrounds have experience of different critical thinking skills?

Subjects/Texts/Sources of data

Questionnaires/interviews

Methods of data collection

Procedures

Methods of analysis

Problems which might be encountered

Appendix 7: Useful language

Useful language: Reporting back

Our group thought the most controversial point was …

Point X provoked the most discussion.

Point X was the most controversial point.

There was some disagreement about point X.

Some people felt …

Most of the group agreed …

Others disagreed …

Useful language: Agreeing and disagreeing

Absolutely. I totally agree.

Yes, that's true, but …

I'm not sure I agree with you there.

I agree up to a point, but …

Not necessarily.

That's a very good point.

Useful language: Signpost expressions (see also Appendix 1)

There are five main points which we consider important for successful study.

Our first point is …

Next, we have put …

Moving onto our third point, …

Fourthly, we think …

And finally, our last point is …

Unit 2

Useful language: Comparing perspectives

From a (teacher's) perspective, …

From the point of view of (the parents), …

If I were (the head teacher of the child's school), I'd probably feel that …

The (child psychologist) would argue that …

Useful language: Summarising a discussion

Summing up your position

We finally all agreed that …

After much consideration, we decided that …

All things considered, we felt that …

On balance, we felt that …

We couldn't reach agreement on this issue. Some of us felt that …, whilst others …

Recognising strong arguments against your position

It's true that …

We recognised that …

We're fully aware that …

One has to acknowledge that …

Qualifying your position

This action should only be taken if …

So, although we agreed with the statement, we stressed that …

Useful language: Chairing a discussion

Getting started

Shall we begin?

Today, we're looking at the following question/topic …

Who would like to begin?

Clarification

So what you mean is …

If I've understood you correctly …

Managing contributions

Thanks, Pete, for your contribution …

OK, Pete, would anyone else like to comment?

Concluding

So, to sum up, …

We're running out of time, so …

Does anyone want to make a final point?

Have I forgotten anything?

Useful language: Referring to an article

This article deals with …

The main point of this article is …

There are three main points discussed in this article.

The article reports that …

It refers to …

The article also gives statistics from …

According to the article/author, …

The article then goes on to say that …

The article argues that …

It quotes …

In my view, the article does not …

It doesn't mention …

Useful language: Exchanging opinions

Asking for opinions

What are your views on this issue?

Do you agree?

Presenting your own opinion

Well, I think …

It seems to me that …

In my view, …

Countering the other person's opinion

I take your point, but …

I understand what you're saying, but …

Well, I'm not sure if that's quite true …

But surely …

Unit 4

Useful language: Clarifying and confirming understanding

Confirming understanding as a listener

So what you're saying is …

So in your view, …

If I understand you correctly, you're saying …

Checking understanding as a speaker

Do you understand what I mean?

Do you follow what I am saying?

Am I making sense?

Showing that you do not understand

I'm not sure I understand what you mean.

I didn't quite follow you. Could you explain that point again, please?

Could you repeat that, please?

Unit 5

Useful language: Referring to data

This graph gives information about …

This chart describes …

This chart clearly shows that …

This line here shows …

As these figures illustrate, …

Useful language: Referring to other speakers

When you say … do you mean that …?

As you said, …

You made an interesting point about …

Following on from that point, …

Regarding what you say about …

Can I also pick up on your point about …?

Those are fair arguments.

You make the point that …

As I said before, …

Useful language: Taking your turn

You want to make a point that is relevant at this moment in the discussion. You need to enter the discussion politely, but firmly:

Can I just come in here?

You want to make a point, but the discussion moves on before you can contribute or finish. You can still make your point later:

To go back to my earlier point, …

Coming back to what John said earlier, …

I think I agree with the point you made earlier, Anne.

You start speaking at the same moment as another student. Both of you stop to let the other speak. It is polite to offer each other the chance to continue:

A: *Sorry, carry on.*

B: *No, go ahead.*

A: *Thanks. I think … [A makes his/her point and then invites B to speak] Sorry, you were going to say …*

B: *Yes, I think …*

You notice that a quiet student is trying to speak, but other students keep speaking first. You can help the quiet student to get the attention of the group:

I think David has been trying to make a point.

David, did you want to make a point?

Unit 8

Useful language: Expressing quantity

Most Nearly all		of those interviewed/questioned ... of the subjects ... of the respondents ...	reported/ stated/ claimed that ...
Approximately Approaching Just under Just over	half a third 50%		

Unit 9

Useful language: Expressing doubt and belief

I don't believe in this/these!

They don't exist.

It can't possibly be true ...

It might be true ...

There might be something in it.

I believe it does work.

I believe it might work.

Appendix 8: Photocopiable handouts

Name of presenter	
Pronunciation of sounds/words	not clear reasonably clear clear very clear
Intonation	not varied quite varied varied
Volume	too quiet appropriate
Speed	too fast too slow appropriate
Eye contact	none too little reasonable good very good

Other comments

Appendix 8b: Discussion review

Participant

Name					
Did you ...	**1**	contribute to the discussion?		Yes	No
		If yes, how much? If no, why not?			
	2	listen and respond to what others said?		Yes	No
	3	encourage others to speak?		Yes	No
	4	refer to any of the points from the articles?		Yes	No
	5	feel the group reached a balanced conclusion, acknowledging different perspectives?		Yes	No
	6	use any of the useful language from this unit?		Yes	No

Chairperson

Name					
Did you ...	**1**	feel that you managed the discussion effectively?		Yes	No
	2	enjoy your role as chairperson?		Yes	No
	3	use any of the 'useful language'?		Yes	No
	4	feel the group reached a balanced conclusion, acknowledging different perspectives?		Yes	No
What was difficult for you as chairperson?					

Name of presenter		
Was the topic clearly identified at the beginning?	Yes	No
Were the main points of the article clearly explained?	Yes	No
Did the presenter give his/her own views on the article?	Yes	No
Did the presenter explain the meaning of any difficult or technical words?	Yes	No
Was the visual aid helpful?	Yes	No
Suggestions for improvement		

Appendix 8d: Discussion review

Group members		
1	**Did everyone in the group contribute to the discussion?**	Yes No
2	**Did group members encourage each other to speak?**	Yes No
3	**How could the group improve the next discussion?**	
4	**Did you check that people understood what you were saying?**	Yes No
5	**Did you indicate when you did not understand?**	Yes No
6	**Did you refer to any of the point from the articles in your discussion?**	Yes No
7	**Were you satisfied with your own participation in the discussion? (Why? Why not?)**	
8	**How could you improve your participation in the next discussion?**	

1	Did everyone in the group contribute to the discussion?	Yes / No
2	Did group members encourage each other to speak?	Yes / No
3	Did speakers refer to points made by other group members?	Yes / No
4	Do you feel the discussion had a sense of direction?	Yes / No
5	How could the group improve the next discussion?	
6	Did you use any of the Useful language for referring to other speakers?	Yes / No
7	Were you satisfied with your participation in the discussion?	Yes / No
	Why? Why not?	
8	How could you improve your participation in the next discussion?	
9	Did your ideas change during the discussion?	Yes / No
	If so, how did they change?	

Appendix 8f: Assessing seminar leader's role: Check list

1	Was the seminar topic appropriate, for example, a topic of interest to the group, and one they could participate in?	Yes / No
	Please comment	

2	Did the seminar leader give enough information about the topic in the beginning?	Yes / No
	Please comment	

3	Did the leader manage the seminar successfully? For example: – keep the discussion going; – allow everyone the opportunity to speak; – ensure one individual did not dominate.	Yes / No
	Please comment	

4	In what way could the seminar discussion have been improved?
	Please comment

| How clearly did the speakers present their ideas? |
| Does it seem like a worthwhile proposal or experiment? |
| Can you see any problems in the experiment/proposal? |
| Overall comment |